# COUNTERMOVE

## When God turns your setback into your comeback

Murry Ray

**Countermove:** *When God turns your setback into your comeback*

Murry Ray



Cover design by Garrett Ray

Printed in the United States of America

ISBN: 978-1-961482-25-8

# Dedication

**To Tom**

**… a brother born for adversity.**

"Blessed are the peacemakers."
Matthew 5:9

# Introduction

I must be the first to confess that I do not count myself to be a great preacher, but I do love great preaching. Over the years, I have been privileged to hear the best preaching in the world. My roots in Pentecost are deep, and my love for Pentecostal preaching is inextricably tied to my heritage. As a child, I remember watching Rev. W.E. Gamblin as he deftly waved his arms while preaching the Word of God. He possessed a graceful gait as he marched back and forth across the platform, declaring truths that became the bedrock of my faith.

The old church on Border Street in Orange, Texas, where he and other great men like Rev. Fred Foster once pastored, is no longer standing. That was the church where my parents were married and where I was dedicated to the Lord. As it was being torn down, a family friend stopped by and retrieved a brick from the rubble of that old House of God. He gave it to my parents who placed it on a credenza in their home. It may seem trite or insignificant, but that old brick remains as a testimony to the history and the heritage that belongs to our family.

When I was nine years old, we began attending the United Pentecostal Church in Bridge City, Texas. I did not realize it at the time, but I was about to be introduced to one of the greatest ministries that God had ever placed within His Church. I'll never forget the first time I met the late Rev. J.W. Harrell. His height notwithstanding, he was a giant in my eyes. I was both afraid and in awe of him. As the years progressed, I came to understand and appreciate the enormity of his ministry and influence in my life. His mentorship, leadership, and friendship have meant more to me than I could ever express. His preaching was unparalleled. His wisdom, unmitigated. His passion for the Kingdom was incomparable. The anointing upon his life was a force itself. I owe him a debt of gratitude that I could never repay. Thank you, Bro. Harrell, for investing in me.

Along the way, there have been others who have taken the time to share their wisdom, skill, and insight with me. The late Rev. George

Joyce, my dear friend and mentor, invested much time in me and placed a love for reading within my heart. The countless hours we spent sitting in his living room discussing Scripture and sermons have forever left an indelible impression upon my life. When he retired from Pastoral Ministry, he gave me most of his library, a treasure I cherish greatly.

Words would fail to express my gratitude to Rev. Richard Price for his influence and friendship in my life. I don't know where I'd be without him. Over the years I have gleaned from his wit and wisdom as much as from his kindness and compassion toward me and toward others. He is a worthy minister of the Gospel. We are family.

I feel like the writer of Hebrews must've felt when he attempted to list the heroes of faith whose legacy was worthy of remembrance. There simply seemed to be too many to name, so he referred to those remaining by saying, "and others." Time would fail me to tell of the "others" in my life: Ron Macey, Ken Gurley, M.J. Moore, Jeff Sanders, B.J. Thomas, E.L. Holley, James Kilgore, James Hughes, Wayne McClain, Wayne Huntley, Rich Price, Tim Gaddy, "and others." To a man, heroes!

I could not thank my family enough for their support and love through the years. My parents instilled within me a love for God. My In-Laws, the best of the best. Jeanine, the light of my life. Madeline and Garrett, the treasures of my heart. Ryan, a blessing, indeed. Alexis, bright and beautiful. Our four grandbabies, Flynn, Heidi Jo, Felicity, and Elowyn Jane bring us more joy than we could have ever imagined. Wherever God leads us. Whatever He calls us to do. Together. Always.

To the wonderful people that I have had the privilege of pastoring over the past 30 years, your faithfulness and support have been an incalculable blessing to me. I owe you each a debt of gratitude that I can never repay.

Murry Ray

# Prologue

This book is for anyone who has ever been caught between conflict and peace, weakness and strength, sickness and health, and all other mortal struggles in life. In moments like these, I have found the contrast more than intriguing. I have found it profoundly inspiring. Through the Scripture, I have watched as God turns our mourning into dancing, sorrow into joy, defeat into victory, and loss into gain. I have witnessed moments when men were down and out, but God lifted them up and brought them back in. I have found that we exist in a paradox. We suffer but are strong. We fall but also rise. We fail but also succeed. We weep but also laugh. It amazes me how the grace of God conspires to turn the tables, always and ever, upon our adversary, as well as our adversities. Like Peter, we are sifted but saved. Like David, we are weak but anointed. Like Luke's "little flock" (Luke 12:32), we are little but loved. In all things pertaining to our lives, it is always "the Father's good pleasure to give to us the Kingdom."

We are connected to both ends of life's spectrum in a unique and powerful way. God does not allow us to be in peril without also covenanting with us through promise. He never allows temptation without an escape mechanism; never gives us burdens without also loading us with blessing. Our circumstances are yoked together with great hopes by a conjunction that is divine. If only we were left to the negative forces and facts that often surround us, we would be of all men most miserable. Yet God attaches to those malignant and melancholy matters of life just one phrase that turns the tide in our favor. Forty to sixty times the Bible uses the phrase, "But God," depending upon what translation is used. Things would not have gone well for many of our scriptural heroes, "But God!" This divine conjunction carried them from peril to power, from death to deliverance, from darkness to light. No matter what the enemy, or life may throw at you, God always has a countermove. According to Merriam-Webster a countermove is a move designed to check, offset, or counter another move. A good chess player knows how to use a counterplay effectively. When trapped, the chess master will use a countermeasure that gives him the advantage over his opponent. Isn’t that exactly where the enemy thinks he has us? Trapped! Defeated! Check-mated! Yet, like a great chess master, our God is always one step ahead. As you read the ensuing pages, may you be reminded that He never leaves His people where life lands them.

# Table of Contents

## *Chapter One*

# We Can't But He Can

> It is easier for a camel to go through the eye of a needle, than for a rich man to enter into the kingdom of God. And they were astonished out of measure, saying among themselves, Who then can be saved? And Jesus looking upon them saith, With men it is impossible, but not with God: for with God all things are possible.
>
> Mark 10:25-27

It has been said that if we will just do what we can, God will do what we can't. I believe that. I am acutely aware of my limitations and inabilities. There are many things that I simply cannot do. The power of my humanity is limited by the weaknesses of my flesh. What an irony that is, for in man there is an immeasurable ability to hope and to dream about things that are beyond himself. In his quest to create and to invent, man always arrives at the stifling abyss of his own limitations. Man has conquered Polio, but there is still no cure for the common cold. He has defeated and made extinct other malicious maladies, but there is no cure for many forms of cancer. We have placed men on the moon and satellites have landed on other planets, but man has yet to find an answer to the current energy troubles of our day.

We have on one hand the ability to do the unthinkable, and yet we are handicapped on the other because of weaknesses in other areas. In our spiritual life, nothing is more frustrating than this knowledge. We pray for things to change, for people to turn their lives around, for miracles to come to pass, but then we recognize that it is humanly impossible to make these things happen. Jesus said we can speak to the mountain, and it must be removed and cast into the midst of the sea. Jesus gave us authority over deadly, spiritual philosophies and the venomous assaults of our adversary. We have the Word of God upon which we stand and declare that God is true and that He is bound by His own word to do that which He promised. We believe in divine healing, spiritual power, apostolic anointing and the gifting of the Spirit. We flex our spiritual muscles once in a while but soon realize that we are just the branches and without the vine we can do nothing.

As a man, even Christ realized that He could do nothing of Himself. His flesh had no power. It was just like ours; it had its limitations. When He had traveled as far as His flesh could take Him, He was tempted by the devil with power and all its allure. When His flesh became weakened at Calvary's crucifixion, He cried out and said, "I thirst!" When that flesh had been beaten and torn beyond recognition; when it could not sustain the loss of blood any longer, Jesus cried out, "It is finished!"

It is interesting that Jesus did not claim to have all power in heaven and in earth until after His resurrection, just before His ascension. Until that time, Jesus only claimed that His power rested in dependence upon His heavenly Father.

It seems to me that with all the shouting about what we have done, we don't have a whole lot to brag about. I cannot save my lost loved ones. I cannot work out all the details of my life and fix everything that falls apart around me. I can't make anyone live for God. I can't decide if you will be saved. I can't make you happy. It is not within my power to cause you to succeed or to fail, to be defeated or to have victory. It is not within any of us to do that. We do not have the power to make all our wishes come true. We can't. We can't do a great many things. We can't, but He can!

A rich young ruler came to Jesus seeking eternal life. His money had gotten him everything; wealth, fame, and good fortune. Perhaps, he was an up-and-coming political figure with  high aspirations. On the surface it seemed he had it all, but he knew there was one thing that he didn't have. He kneeled before Jesus and asked, "What must I do to inherit eternal life?" Jesus said, "You have to keep the commandments." He replied that he had done so since he was a child.

The commandments were not his problem. His value system was not in order. Jesus told him to sell all that he had, give it to the poor, take up a cross, and follow Him. But the young man had too much — too much acceptance and affluence, too much fame and notoriety, too much ambition, too much fear of what people might say. Notwithstanding, for all that he did have there was something that he had too little of. The young ruler did not have enough appreciation for the life to come. He did not value eternal life nearly as much as he valued his present life. The temporal world around him held more appeal than the eternal glory that he had inquired about. We are left with the impression that eternal life was only something else to be added to his list of achievements, something to make his resume look better. He trusted riches over redemption. To be saved, all a person has to essentially do is value the life to come more than the life they now live. That perspective changes everything. Sadly, this rich young ruler risked being lost for all eternity because he lacked value of eternal things.

Jesus watches him walk away, turns to those still gathered around and says something amazing. "How hard is it for them that trust in riches to enter into the kingdom of God?" Before they could reply,

He answers His own question saying, "It is easier for a camel to go through the eye of a needle, than for a rich man to enter into the kingdom of God." Amazed, they queried, "Who then can be saved?" And Jesus looking upon them said, "With men it is impossible, but not with God: for with God all things are possible."

The passing of a camel through the eye of a needle is figurative; it represents that which is impossible. It means that it cannot be done. Jesus said, "There isn't a man alive who can make this happen." With all that man can do, there comes a point where he can do no more. There are some things that reach beyond the scope of his abilities. There are some extremes to which he cannot go. With man this is impossible.

My pastor once preached, "God knows how to thread a needle!" You can try all day long to force a square peg through a round hole, but you will never accomplish the task without destroying something. That is why men will usually give up long before an impossible task is completed. But God knows how to thread the needle!

This principle doesn't just apply to wealthy people. It applies to all of us who have ever tried to do something that seemed impossible. If you have ever prayed for someone who was in an impossible position in life and lived with the agony of watching them wallow in the mire continually, this chapter is for you. If you have ever prayed for a situation that seemed to only get worse, God is speaking a word to you. If you have ever felt the pressures of life closing in on you, caving in around you, and thought there was no possible way out to safety, I encourage you to pay close attention to what He is saying.

Every time I read this story, I am reminded of a man I once knew. For years, his wife and children lived in an impossible situation. The man had run as far from God as a man could get. He rebelled against everything he had been taught as a child. He ran from everything that common sense told him he needed to do. His wife stayed faithful to God and to him for all those years. She carried that impossibility with her everywhere she went. I cannot tell you the conversations that she and I had over the years about what to do. It was one of the most impossible situations I have ever seen.

Then something extreme happened: God began to thread that needle. As the man passed through the eye of it, cancer invaded his body, but the Spirit of God invaded his soul! For the last several months of his life he was at every church service that he could get to. Finally, one night, he prayed through to the Holy Ghost. From that night until he passed away, he'd get tapes of sermons and share them with people. He invited his friends to come to church. He made things right.

Since he died instead of being healed, some may not view this as a positive testimony. You can say whatever you want about it: call it extreme, deem it all unnecessary, diminish the miracle. But heaven is going to be sweeter for his family because he is already there. God knows how to thread the needle!

There are impossible things that we can't do, but He can. So, why not let Him? The question is not, "Will God work?" The question is, "Who will let Him?"

Don't place so much value on the temporal that you hinder God from doing something eternal. "The eyes of the LORD run to and fro throughout the whole earth, to show himself strong in the behalf of them whose heart is perfect toward him" (2 Chroniccles 16:9). Jesus would have worked great miracles for Jerusalem, but they would not let Him. They missed their hour for deliverance. They could not deliver themselves out of the bondage that had enslaved them, but He could. If only they had let Him work.

I was going to omit this chapter from this book because I wasn't really "feeling" it. But early one morning the Lord woke me up and the first thing that crossed my mind was this Word. I tried to go back to sleep, but for a few moments all I could hear was, "You can't, but

I can!" The Spirit is speaking a word of encouragement and power into our hearts. Don't worry about doing what you can't do. Don't worry about the impossibility that stands before you. Don't worry about the limitations you face. Don't be anxious about the negative report. God's got this! That situation you can't change. That person you can't seem to win. That bill you can't pay. That job you can't get. That future you can't embrace. That hurt you can't get over. That sorrow you can't replace. That offense you can't let go of. That wall you can't move. That needle you can't thread.

God woke me up early so I would remind someone that He can! He can change a person's heart. He can heal every hurt. He can produce promotion. He can give you joy for sorrow. He can knock the wall down. He can heal the offense. He can provide the means. He can change the situation. He can thread the needle!

Don't make the fatal mistake of overvaluing the present and undervaluing the eternal. You can do like the rich young ruler and walk away full handed and empty hearted. Or you can walk away empty handed, and full hearted! All God was asking of the young man is really all God is asking of you — just empty your hands so He can fill your heart. Give your impossibility to God and watch Him turn it into a possibility. He can!

Many years ago, I was introduced to the story of a father and son team that has defied all the odds. "Team Hoyt," as they are often referred to, were an amazing pair. Their story is more than the simple retelling of how two determined athletes participated and completed one of the world's most grueling events: the Ironman. It is a love story, one that expresses the deep devotion that a father has for his son. Their biography, "It's Only A Mountain," details their life and the challenges they had to face and overcome. The Hoyt family has conquered many mountains, the first of which they faced when Rick, their eldest son, was born with cerebral palsy. A non-verbal quadriplegic, Rick's life would be filled with impossibilities. He would never run like other boys, never ride a bike like his brothers, never swim in a pool on hot summer days. All of the things that boys are born to do were impossible for him to accomplish. Or, were they?

Dick Hoyt, Rick's father, was a very accomplished athlete in his own right. But above that, he was a man of determination and devotion, a man of dedication. In 2008, I was privileged to attend a small gathering where Dick Hoyt would be speaking. Having read their story, I was eager to hear him. At the close of the evening, I was honored to meet Mr. Hoyt and to speak with him briefly. One of the most cherished publications in my library is an autographed copy of their book, which he gave me that night. Early on, he decided that he would not allow anything to stand in Rick's way of having as normal a life as possible. The Hoyts were told by doctors that Rick would never be able to speak or to walk. "Just put him in an institution and forget about him," they said. Dick and Judy Hoyt refused their advice and took their son home.

As time passed, the Hoyts noticed that although Rick could not speak, he was learning to communicate with his eyes. While his body seemed broken, his mind was not. After sharing their story with a psychologist at the Children's Hospital in Boston, he gave them some different advice from previous physicians. He said, "Treat him just like every other child." The Hoyts took his advice and soon Dick was taking his son boating, fishing, sledding, even swimming. Judy taught him the alphabet. His education was in full swing.

By the age of 12, Rick was learning to communicate with slight nods and smiles. While this method worked well enough with his closest family members, Rick was still not able to fully express himself as he desired. The Hoyts teamed up with a group of engineers from Tufts University to build a machine that would allow Rick to communicate with the rest of the world. What came next was a game changer. The team soon developed what the Hoyts came to call "The Hope Machine." This device would allow Rick to spell out words and form sentences on a computer screen by tapping his head against an attached headpiece.

Family members began a friendly wager as to what his first words would be. "I love you, Mom," or "Hi, Dad" were the favorites to win. Much to their surprise, Rick's first words were, "Go Bruins!" This was a reference to the Boston Bruins who were playing in the finals for the Stanley Cup. Rick had developed a love for sports.

At age 13, he heard about a five-mile charity run to benefit a lacrosse player who had been paralyzed in an accident. He enlisted his father's help, and they entered their first race. "Dad, when we run, I feel like my disability disappears," Rick said after they completed the competition. Together, they made it their mission to race as much as possible. By developing a specialized wheelchair, Dick was able to push his son while running. Soon he developed a bicycle with a raised seat for Rick to sit in while his dad pedaled and steered the bike. When it came time to swim in a triathlon, Dick placed him in a specialized raft that he would harness himself to and pull Rick through the water. In a career that spanned 41 years, the two conquered over 1,100 endurance events worldwide, including 36 Boston Marathon finishes, countless local 5K and 10K races, more than 70 marathons, and multiple Ironman triathlons. Team Hoyt became a racing legend.

Your story and mine are much like Team Hoyt's. Born with a nature that defies us to overcome it, we are often challenged to rise above its limitations. There are so many restraints within us, so many facts that halt our progress. We simply cannot run this race on our own. How can we ever hope to cross the finish line when we can't even cross the starting line? I will tell you how. By trusting in a Father Who can and Who will! We are yoked with Him as a team.

As I close this chapter, I am reminded of a story told by Chick Moorman, an American educator and author with over 40 years of classroom experience. It's called the "I Can't Funeral."

Donna's fourth-grade classroom looked like many others I had seen in the past. Students sat in five rows of six desks. The teacher's desk was in the front and faced the students. The bulletin board featured student work. In most respects it appeared to be a typically traditional elementary classroom. Yet something seemed different that day I entered it for the first time. There seemed to be an undercurrent of excitement.

Donna was a veteran small-town, Michigan schoolteacher only two years away from retirement. In addition, she was a volunteer participant in a country-wide staff development project I had organized and facilitated. The training focused on language arts ideas that would empower students to feel good about themselves and take charge of their lives. Donna's job was to attend training sessions and implement the concepts being presented. My job was to make classroom visitations and encourage implementation.

I took an empty seat in the back of the room and watched. All the students were working on a task, filling a sheet of notebook paper with thoughts and ideas. The ten-year-old student closest to me was filling her page with "I Cant's."

"I can't kick the soccer ball past second base."
"I can't do long division with more than three numerals."
"I can't get Debbie to like me."

Her page was half full and she showed no signs of letting up. She worked on with determination and persistence.

I walked down the row glancing at students' papers. Everyone was writing sentences, describing things they couldn't do.

"I can't do ten push-ups."
"I can't hit one over the left-field fence."
"I can't eat only one cookie."

By this time, the activity engaged my curiosity, so I decided to check with the teacher to see what was going on. As I approached her, I noticed that she too was busy writing. I felt it best not to interrupt.

"I can't get John's mother to come in for a teacher conference."
"I can't get my daughter to put gas in the car."
"I can't get Alan to use words instead of fists."

Thwarted in my efforts to determine why students and teacher were dwelling on the negative instead of writing the more positive "I can" statements, I returned to my seat and continued my observations. Students wrote for another ten minutes. Most filled their page. Some started another.

"Finish the one you're on and don't start a new one," were the instructions Donna used to signal the end of the activity. Students were then instructed to fold their papers in half and bring them to the front. When students reached the teacher's desk, they placed their "I Can't" statements into an empty shoe box.

When all of the student papers were collected, Donna added hers. She put the lid on the box, tucked it under her arm and headed out the door and down the hall. Students followed the teacher. I followed the students.

Halfway down the hall the procession stopped. Donna entered the custodian's room, rummaged around and came out with a shovel. Shovel in one hand, shoe box in the other, Donna marched the students out of the school to the farthest corner of the playground. There they began to dig.

They were going to bury their "I Can'ts!" The digging took over ten minutes because most of the fourth graders wanted a turn. When the hole approached three-feet deep, the digging ended. The box of "I Can'ts" was placed in position at the bottom of the hole and quickly covered with dirt.

Thirty-one 10 and 11-year-olds stood around the freshly dug grave site. Each had at least one page full of "I Can'ts" in the shoe box, three-feet-under. So did their teacher.

At this point Donna announced, "Boys and girls, please join hands and bow your heads." The students complied. They quickly formed a circle around the grave, creating a bond with their hands. They lowered their heads and waited. Donna delivered the eulogy.

"Friends, we gather today to honor the memory of 'I Can't.' While he was with us on earth, he touched the lives of everyone, some more than others. His name, unfortunately, has been spoken in every public building—schools, city halls, state capitols and yes, even the White House."

"We have provided 'I Can't' with a final resting place and a headstone that contains his epitaph. He is survived by his brothers and sister, 'I Can,' 'I Will,' and 'I'm going to right Away.' They are not as well-known as their famous relative and are certainly not as strong and powerful yet. Perhaps someday, with your help, they will make an even bigger mark on the world."

"May 'I Can't' rest in peace and may everyone present pick up their lives and move forward in his absence. Amen."

As I listened to the eulogy, I realized that these students would never forget this day. The activity was symbolic, a metaphor for life. It was a right-brain experience that would stick in the subconscious and conscious mind forever.

Writing "I Can'ts," burying them, and hearing the eulogy. That was a major effort on the part of this teacher. And she wasn't done yet.

At the conclusion of the eulogy, she turned the students around, marched them back into the classroom, and held a wake.

They celebrated the passing of "I Can't" with cookies, popcorn, and fruit juices. As part of the celebration, Donna cut out a large tombstone from butcher paper. She wrote the words "I Can't" at the top and put RIP in the middle. The date was added at the bottom.

The paper tombstone hung in Donna's classroom for the remainder of the year. On those rare occasions when a student forgot and said, "I can't," Donna simply pointed to the RIP sign. The student then remembered that "I Can't" was dead and chose to rephrase the statement.

> I wasn't one of Donna's students. She was one of mine. Yet that day I learned an enduring lesson from her.
>
> Now, years later, whenever I hear the phrase, "I can't," I see images of that fourth-grade funeral. Like the students, I remember that "I Can't" is dead.

Perhaps, we should have a funeral, too. Maybe it's time to bury that same old attitude and replace it with, "I can do all things through Christ who strengthens me" (Philippians 4:13 NKJV).

Teacher Talk: What It Really Means by Chick Moorman & Nancy Weber; Personal Power Press (Bay City, Michigan) January 1989

.

## *Chapter Two*

# Weak But Anointed

> And the king said unto his servants, Know ye not that there is a prince and a great man fallen this day in Israel? And I am this day weak, though anointed king; and these men the sons of Zeruiah be too hard for me: the Lord shall reward the doer of evil according to his wickedness.
>
> II Samuel 3:38-39

Having been anointed as Saul's successor, David had to wait many years to become Israel's King. During much of that time he was forced to live in exile. King Saul persistently pursued him, so his life was in danger on a daily basis.

Eventually, a band of men gathered around him and became a make-shift army that protected the land from foreign foes. These "mighty men of valor" stood up for those who were disenchanted, disenfranchised, and indebted to cruel masters. They devoted their lives to David. From cave to cave and conflict to conflict, they followed him as he fought his way to the crown he was anointed to wear.

David lived this way until that fateful day when Saul was killed in battle on Mt. Gilboa. An Amalekite brought the head of the fallen king to David thinking he would be rewarded for his action. Instead, David put him to death. Perhaps a warning to us all that, "Doing what we have the right to do may not be the right thing to do!"

What ensued next is a sordid tale of political ambitions gone wild. David's own kinsmen at once recognized him as the leader of their clan, and he, in Hebron, began to reign over Judah and the southern part of the country. But the mass of the nation had not yielded their loyalties to him, especially Abner, the commander-in-chief of Saul's standing army. Instead, he set up Ishbosheth as the successor of Saul. The kingdom became divided. David was the acknowledged head of Judah and Benjamin, and Ishbosheth became the master of the larger part of the territory, the ten northern tribes. Ungodly ambition is a hard taskmaster, and Abner was consumed and controlled by it. When he and Ishbosheth had a falling out, Abner approached David with a plan to remove the northern king. Lurking in the shadows, David's lead man, Joab, hears this and fears he will lose his position. He follows Abner back to Hebron, and luring him outside the city walls, slays him in cold blood.

It is a fact that leaders cannot always control or contain their subjects, and David was forced to deal with Joab in such a way that the king's hands were free of Abner's blood. David did not, after all, have anything to do with Joab's actions and lamented Abner's death. He pronounced judgment upon Joab, even though there was really nothing he could do to him. It seems that Joab was within his rights as "the avenger of blood" to slay Abner. (Abner had slain Joab's brother Asahel in battle.)

The cold and calloused heart of Joab was calculating and cunning. He had gotten away with murder and seemed to have no remorse at all. Even though he was David's nephew, he was nothing like his uncle. His heart was not after God's heart; it seems that Joab was driven by deadly ambition. His heart was after power.

Nonetheless, David made him walk in the funeral procession next to himself. As David sang a poetic, yet mournful dirge over the lifeless body of Abner, Joab was unmoved and unremorseful. And it is this moment that causes David to lament, "The sons of Zeruiah are too hard-hearted for me. They are calloused and cold-blooded. I can't stand to be associated with them. Yet, there isn't much I can do about them, either."

It is then that David makes both a confession and a proclamation. He said, "I am weak, but I am still anointed." He was faint, but not faint-hearted. He was frail, but not falling apart. His capacities were diminished, but His covenant was not destroyed. He was stressed, but still blessed. He was disappointed but remained anointed.

Never underestimate the power of the anointing in your life. The Lord spoke to Paul and said, "... my strength is made perfect in weakness..." Paul replied by saying, "... I will glory in weakness that the power of Christ may rest upon me" (II Corinthians 12:9) The anointing is powerful! Jesus Christ was "The Anointed One." He was God in flesh doing what was impossible for flesh to do. He was strength made perfect in weakness.

The anointing allows us to accomplish through the Spirit what cannot be done in the flesh. Every child of God is anointed in Him. Whomever God appoints He also anoints.

Yet, there is a truth that must be understood. You can be anointed and still grow weak. Weakness and anointing often stand together. You may be destined to fulfill a grand purpose and yet not have strength enough to accomplish it within yourself. God may want to use you to do great things, but you will often feel utterly helpless to accomplish them.

Some of God's greatest servants have felt as if they were, in fact, God's weakest servants. Elijah despaired. Samson had his eyes put out. Moses made mistakes. Joseph was thrown into a pit. Peter sank in despair. Thomas doubted. Martha wept. Mary was confused. Lazarus died. The best of men are men at best.

Sometimes we have weak faith. We need help with our unbelief. We need encouragement to believe. There are days when we sigh and cry; days we are worried and woeful. There are, indeed, moments when our faith is less than a grain of mustard seed. There are times when our hope is weak. The political outlook isn't very good. The moral outlook isn't much better. Things society embraces offer no brighter future. Even the best of us is subject to fear and discouragement because of the bleak outlook of the present. Often the heart of God's children is tempted to say, "We might as well eat, drink and be merry for tomorrow we die" (Luke 12:19).

But I challenge you to get a hold of this grand truth. Your weakness does not negate His strength. Your feelings don't erase the anointing. You may feel as weak as a beggar, but the fact remains that you are an anointed king. Your faith may feel as if it lacks the power to move a pebble, much less a mountain, but don't forget that you are still anointed. Just because the papers are sealed in the vault doesn't mean the inheritance isn't yours. You may not feel it, but the anointing is still present.

Sometimes it seems that our best efforts fall way short of the mark. A preacher preaches and wonders if his sermons have made any difference. A mother prays and worries that her prayers have fallen short. A father works and wonders if his labor will accomplish anything. A student is surrounded by wickedly perverse ideas and ungodly behaviors. They feel as if they are just one rock trying to stop the crooked currents from overtaking their school. Sometimes we shout with Solomon, "Vanity of vanities! All is vanity!"

I say, "Don't let your weakness discount your uniqueness. God has called you and He will secure you!" Whom He appoints, He also anoints. You may be weak but don't forget, you are still anointed.

You may not be where you want to be, but your position doesn't lessen your anointing. David was forced to hide in a cave. The Adullam cave was full of fear and disappointment. His enemies sought him out. The Philistines rose up against him. Saul pursued him. The scent of that cave wreaked with the odor of defeat. The acrid smell of that forgotten cavern filled the atmosphere with the stench of a dying purpose. But there were times, when the wind was just right, David could catch the scent of something heavenly. Above it all were steady reminders of who David was. For at the right moment, he could smell the lingering aroma of his anointing.

You may be standing in a place you never thought you'd ever stand. Your difficulties are as diverse as they are detrimental. Burdens may be as heavy as the light of day is bright. Fears may be more intimidating than anything you've ever experienced. Hurts may be more painful than any wound you've ever had. Realities may be harsher than any you've ever faced.

But if you exercise your senses, you will pick up the scent of a past anointing. Your position in life doesn't change your position with God. Your problem doesn't cancel your promise. What you face on earth doesn't change where you stand in heaven. What you feel here doesn't negate what is known there. Where you stand with them doesn't change how you stand with Him!

Philistine pillars still collapse when weak Samsons declare their anointing. An exiled Moses is made to understand that wherever God shows up it is Holy Ground. You may be standing in an unemployment line, but you're still anointed. You may be sitting in a doctor's waiting room, but you are still anointed. You didn't get the promotion, but you're still anointed. Your family problems have surmounted, but you still dwell in the realm of an anointing. You are standing in a place of pain and confusion, but you're still anointed. You may find yourself somewhere in life you have never been before, but you are still anointed.

Don't underestimate the power of your anointing. Everything may stand in opposition against you, but don't forget who you are. David was surrounded by people who felt very strongly that he had no right to be the king. Saul's household was against him. His own nephews behaved in such a way that he could not do much with them. The Philistines certainly didn't want him leading God's people. They had too much to gain by a weak Israel. He faced opposition to his purpose at every turn.

But don't count David out. He was uniquely anointed and divinely appointed. God picked him for the palace. He matched the man to the mission. God called him, and God would equip him. Even when he was weak, he was still the anointed King.

Some people will not support your appointing because they don't understand your anointing. They don't see what God sees. They don't know what God knows. They don't desire what God desires. Don't be discouraged when people refuse to support you. Don't lose heart when people criticize you. Don't give up when the crowd rejects you. Lack of approval is not the same as lack of anointing. They crucified Jesus, but He was still the Anointed One. You may be wobbling beneath the load of your cross, but that doesn't take your anointing away.

Your weakness does not remove your purpose. It does not keep you from reigning over every situation. It will not deter your destiny. It will not devour your increase. It will not steal your joy, diminish your faith, or crush your hopes. It won't stop God from moving on your behalf, and it won't keep you from obtaining victory. You're just weak. You're not dead. You're wounded, not defeated. You still have an anointing.

Strength is made perfect in weakness. Anointing brings power. To anoint means to "smear or rub into." Sheep were anointed to protect them from blood-sucking insects. Shields were anointed to preserve them and to ensure their longevity in battle. Officials were anointed as a sign of consecration to their calling. The anointing is not a small dab of something supernatural; it's something engrained within your spiritual being that isn't easily removed. The anointing protects you from things that rob you of life. It ensures you in the day of battle. It consecrates you against the day of temptation.

The anointing is divine enablement to accomplish the purpose of God. No wonder Paul said, "I can do all things through Christ who strengthens me!" (Philippians 4:13 NKJV). Don't count yourself out just yet. You may be weak, but you are still anointed!

*Chapter Three*

# Unexpected But Divine

> Oh that thou wouldest rend the heavens, that thou wouldest come down, that the mountains might flow down at thy presence, As when the melting fire burneth, the fire causeth the waters to boil, to make thy name known to thine adversaries, that the nations may tremble at thy presence! When thou didst terrible (awesome) things which we looked not for, thou camest down, the mountains flowed down at thy presence. For since the beginning of the world men have not heard, nor perceived by the ear, neither hath the eye seen, O God, beside thee, what he hath prepared for him that waiteth for him.
>
> Isaiah 64:1-4

As a source of encouragement in difficult times, we often look back to see how the Lord has dealt with us in the past. Tracing God's track record gives us hope for current circumstances in life.

As you turn through the pages of your history with God, you quickly see that God is consistent, if nothing else. There is no variableness in Him. There is no altering of His nature, no changing of His character.

What He was, He is — What He is, He always will be. It's what the Scripture means when it says that He is the same yesterday, today and forever. Immutable, unchanging, infallible, unerring: not simply in one case, but in all cases, He is the same. The very essence of God is that He is without variation from eternity to eternity. What endures does not change and what changes does not endure. Perishing things cannot support the soul.

The Psalmist said to God, "Thou art the same, and thy years shall have no end!" He is the same. The same in nature. The same in will. The same in way. The same in wisdom. The same in power. The same in purpose. Year after year, throughout all eternity, He is the same.

The repetitive nature of His righteousness means that God has always done right, is doing right, and shall continue to do right. He has done right by both men and angels. He has done right by both heaven and earth. He has done right by the righteous and the unrighteous. He did right in the Old Testament, and He has done right in the New Testament. He has done right by Israel, and He has done right by the Church. He has done right in history, and He is doing right in the present. He will do right in the future. In every dispensation that has come, He has done right. In every dispensation to come, He shall do right. In time He has done right, and in eternity He will do right.

In medieval times, our ancestors were governed by kings. They lived with an attitude that declared, "The king can do no wrong." We know how foolish that was for many kings did many wicked things. But the King of Kings can do no wrong.

His record is clean and clear. He did no wrong in the Garden. He did no wrong in the Flood. He did no wrong under the Law. He does no wrong under grace. He is light and in Him there is no darkness. Men have falsely accused Him, but He is innocent. Men have blamed Him for things that He has not done, and though He stands silent before His accusers and executioners, He is blameless, faultless, and guiltless. He has neither spot nor wrinkle; no blemish or shortcoming. He is truth; therefore, nothing false can reside within Him. Jesus is the Lamb slain from the foundation of the world. The lamb offered in the Old Testament was perfect. Pilate looked Christ over closely. He scrutinized what few words Jesus uttered. He examined the testimonies of eyewitnesses that testified against Him. He looked Christ eye to eye, face to face, and finally concluded what angels have known all along, "I find no fault in Him!"

It is my desire to help you understand that God can transform your situation into a blessed hope. If history does indeed repeat itself, then you have a great assurance. What God has been to you in your past, He will be to you in your future. If He has been your deliverer, He will always be your deliverer. If He was your Savior and is your Savior, then He will always be your Savior. If He made a way out of no way once, He will make a way out of no way twice — even more. If He brought you out once, He will bring you out once again. If He showed up yesterday, He will show up again today.

Isaiah prayed, "Lord, look down from heaven." Then he prayed, "Come down from heaven." In the middle of that he prayed, "Rend the heavens." So desperate was Israel's situation that Isaiah shouted, "Rip the sky apart if you have to but come to where we are. We are in a desperate struggle. Cause the canopy between heaven and earth to be torn in two so that you can descend into this dimension."

Isaiah said, "In the year King Uzziah died I saw the Lord, high and lifted up. His train filled the Temple." In that day, the prophet seems to rejoice that God was on His throne. His victory was complete. His power was intact. His position was secure. In that situation, God was high and lifted up. I, too, am glad God is in heaven. But in this instance, Isaiah isn't looking for a God who dwells in heaven. He is looking for a God who dwells on Earth. So, he prayed, "Tear down the curtain of glory that separates us from one another and meet us at the point of our need."

When God got ready to descend to man's level, He did just that. At His crucifixion, the veil in the Temple was rent in two. That veil was nearly 60 feet tall and 4 inches thick. When Christ died for us, the veil was ripped apart from the top all the way down to the bottom. Man was not rending the heavenly veil, God was. Man was not pulling the canopy back and asking, "God, are you up there?" God was peering through the torn top shouting, "I'm coming down there!" The glory of God is not that He met us at the location of our lodging but that He meets us at the habitation of our heart. If Christ on earth among us was awesome, then Christ dwelling within us is incredibly awesome. Unexpected but divine!

I wonder if you, too, need a God on Earth? You rejoice because He is in Heaven. You shout because He sits upon the circle of the Earth. You praise Him because Heaven is His throne and Earth is His footstool, but what you really need is for Him to walk through the door of your heart and be near. Trust His track record. If He left the splendor of Heaven once He will leave it again. Isaiah was no better than you. He was a man of unclean lips, but God still came down to where he was. Unexpected but divine.

God will show up. He showed up for Israel in Egypt, at the Red Sea, and at Marah. He showed up for Elijah at Mt. Carmel. He showed up for Ezekiel in a valley of dry bones. He showed up for Israel at Jericho. He showed up for Jeremiah, Elisha, Amos, and Micah. He even showed up in a manger. He showed up when the disciples tossed their last item overboard in order to keep the ship afloat. He showed up when Peter gave up and went back to his old life of fishing. He showed up when a demoniac had given up all hope of ever being delivered. He showed up when Lazarus was in the grave. When Mary was weeping in wonder about his disappearance from the tomb, He showed up. When the disciples were hungry, when Thomas's doubts had just about gotten the best of him, when a multitude grew too hungry to travel, He showed up. When a disgraced woman needed Him the most, when 120 were gathered in the Upper Room, He showed up. One day He will show up in the clouds of glory.

He will show up in power. He will show up in mercy. He will show up in glory and in grace. He will show up with healing in His wings, with an answered prayer. He will show up with forgiveness and salvation. He will show up in peace.

You may not be expecting a divine visitation, but I believe that one is on its way. Didn't He say, "Where two or three are gathered together in my name, I will be there in the midst of them?" His record is impeccable. He will show up.

When God shows up, things begin to happen. He is full of divine surprises. Isaiah recalled that God performed, "Awesome things that they did not expect" (Is. 64:3 NIV). When God shows up, He always surprises men by what He does. Even at times when the expectations of men have been great, God has far exceeded them. Men have feared dark things only to discover that when God comes, He does something completely wondrous for them. Jacob lost Joseph and said, "All these things are against me." But God was doing awesome things that Jacob did not even expect. He was strategically placing Joseph in position to save his family one day. He was doing "terrible things," which Jacob looked not for.

When Israel stood before the Red Sea, they expected to be marched en masse back to the land of Egypt. They did not expect God to show up and do what He did. If they did have any expectation of deliverance, it does not seem that they expected to walk through the Red Sea on dry ground. What a surprise when God parted the waters and they marched through in victory. In the desert they expected to be scorched by the sun. They did not expect a glory cloud to cover them from its piercing heat. They expected to be at the mercy of the desert's darkness, but God illuminated their tent city — like no other city has ever been lit — with the fiery pillar of His presence. When they got hungry, they expected some kind of provision. They never dreamed that the skies would open and heaven would pour out its bread upon them in the form of manna. They grew thirsty and expected to find water somewhere but not from a rock. They came to a swollen Jordan River and just on the other side was their Promised Land. They expected to get across somehow. They did not expect to cross on dry ground. The priest shouldered the Ark of the Covenant, and when their feet touched the water, the river began to roll back.

When they marched around Jericho, they knew something was going to happen. I seriously doubt they expected the walls to fall. But a divine hand rattled the foundation of Jericho, and the walls came tumbling down. God did awesome things that they were not expecting because when He shows up, He always has a surprise in store.

When the multitude was hungry, they did not expect to be fed out of one little boy's lunch sack. When the disciples needed money to pay taxes, they did not expect to find it in a fish's mouth. When the leper came back to thank Jesus for healing him, he did not expect to also be made whole. When the woman was thrown into the dust at Jesus' feet, she did not expect to go home that day alive, well, and forgiven. When Peter stepped out of the boat, none of the disciples expected him to walk on water. When Mary and the other women went to the tomb, they did not expect to find it empty. When Thomas entered the house, he did not expect to see Jesus. When Paul was on his way to Damascus, he did not expect to run into Him either.

I believe that you are about to enter a place where God is going to shatter all your expectations. But don't worry about it, because He is going to exceed them in such a way that what you thought would happen will pale in comparison to what actually happens. Isaiah said mountains began to melt, waters began to boil, nations trembled, and adversaries realized His presence when God showed up.

I speak a prophetic word to someone right now. Situations that seem immovable are about to melt away. People who once turned a deaf ear are about to pay attention. An enemy that wouldn't quit is about to give up. God is going to show Himself strong on your behalf.
I speak a word of encouragement. God is about to show up in your

life. He has a few surprises up His sleeve. He is going to bless you in ways you haven't thought of. He is going to open doors you didn't even know existed. He is going to provide something you didn't realize that you needed. He is going to work in ways that will amaze you.

How do I know? How can I be so sure? Because His track record says so. His history is impeccable. His past promises say so. Don't give up. Don't doubt. Don't quit. Something unexpected but divine is on its way.

## *Chapter Four*

# Sifted But Saved

> And the Lord said, Simon, Simon, behold, Satan hath desired to have you, that he may sift you as wheat: But I have prayed for thee, that thy faith fail not: and when thou art converted, strengthen thy brethren.
>
> Luke 22:31-32

Within the economy of God, there is an often-overlooked process that we cannot afford to ignore. Historically, we find that God has regularly allowed His people to be put through a sifting process.

In the Book of Amos, the Lord spoke directly to Israel and told them He was going to sift them like corn that is placed within a sieve. Among the nations, He sifted His own saints. It was a painful, violent, and disturbing process that separated them from others around them. Among the heathen, the unbeliever, and the idolater, God created a division between what was problematic and what was productive. God separated the wheat from the chaff, His people from the world, the righteous from the unrighteous.

The shaking and sifting seemed to be unprofitable for those enduring it, but for God's people it opened the door for a great promise. The Lord said, "I will sift you, but not the least grain shall fall to the ground" (Amos 9:9). No doubt there were some that were destroyed, but nothing of value to the Lord was lost. Not one of His children was harmed in the sifting process. In fact, the sifting only increased their worth and value. They were sifted but saved.

In the twilight of His most crushing hour, Christ watched as the sifting process began to take shape among His inner circle. The love and loyalty of His followers was being tested and challenged at every level. The sneers and evil attitudes of the Pharisees were taking more definite shape, expressing themselves in flaming outbursts of hatred and scorn. Many of His followers were deserting Him. The disciples themselves were afraid, and the enemies of Christ were celebrating the imminent downfall of this man from Nazareth.

His death had already been determined. The mob was already forming. The betrayer's feet were on their way to close the deal. As the storm clouds gathered, the remaining disciples gather around their Savior in an effort to protect Him. Peter became emboldened in his zeal to keep harm from coming to Jesus. "I will defend you to the death!" he vowed. A promise he tried to make good on when he later cut off the ear of one of the men who came to take Jesus away. His pledge was not the prattle of a child: Jesus knew Peter meant what he said. But that isn't how the scenario was meant to play out. Jesus was going to teach Simon a powerful principle and reveal to him one of the greatest promises ever made.

In that moment, Jesus parted the curtain of the immediate future and gave us an insight that we need to get a hold of. "Simon, Simon, Satan has desired to have you that he may sift you as wheat!" Simon had no idea how close his enemy had encamped to him.

I suspect that like Job, Peter knew not that Satan was trying to cut a deal with God. His one desire, his utmost intention, all of Hell's focus was on Simon Peter that day. If the enemy could get to him for just a little while. If he could just torment him relentlessly for a few hours. If only he could harass him at will. If he could make him believe he was worthless. If he could just sift him. It was no strange desire — the enemy would like nothing more than to do the same to all of God's children.

That's what Satan desires to do to everyone that belongs to God. The sinister one is of the sifting sort. The destroyer wants to destroy. The expression of an evil heart is always destruction. An evil heart will fight itself. It will war against the things that it loves. Be careful lest an evil heart of unbelief spring up within you. That's the kind of heart Satan possesses.

If the devil could, he would crush every Christian and every cause that dares to oppose him. He would grind every church, every believer, every missionary, every preacher, and every saint into dust. He would hush the mouth of every singer, silence every preacher, and quench the zeal of every Christian. If he could, he would create chaos and havoc in every church. Wreck and ruin, destruction and desolation are his calling cards. If he could, he would sift you in an effort to destroy you.

The truth is, we are often sifted by Satan. But the good news is that he can only do so much. He can't do anything without the permission of God. He wanted to destroy Job, but he had to get permission before he could even touch his life. Even when God allowed him to work in Job's life, the devil was on a very short leash. When Moses died, the devil wanted his body, but God hid it, and the devil could not find it.

I want to tell you a little secret about the enemy of your soul. He can only do so much. He is not equal with God. He cannot create or control the world. He is not on the same playing field as God. He is under God's dominion and power. He really is nothing more than a beggar at the footstool of God's throne.

To be sure, he causes a lot of trouble. But remember that he can only tempt men to do evil. He is an influencer, a manipulator. He cannot make you do anything. He can only tempt you to yield to sin. He cannot force his will upon you. He cannot destroy you if God wants to save you.

Men have often wondered why God would allow the devil to even do that. But when you think about it, it really does make sense. A world without temptation would be a world without any merit. Without temptation, we may be innocent, but we could never be righteous. Innocence is untested and untried goodness, but righteousness is a goodness that has been tested, tried, and proven. Being innocent means you're naïve to evil. Being righteous means you've faced it and walked away in victory. Innocence is the absence of temptation; righteousness is the conquest of it.

An untempted person is like a plant grown in a greenhouse. They are protected and provided for. They have been shielded from the excessive cold and frost of a wild and wintry world. But the proven Christian is like an oak on the mountain that has overcome the winds and rains, the snows and droughts that have come its way. They grow stronger and stronger because they have been strained and stressed by times of tension. God allows temptation to weave His wonder working power into our lives.

Temptation is God's way of growing great character, great lives, and great souls. The sifting of Satan is the refiner's fire that burns away the dross so the gold can shine more brightly and purely. It is like the machinery that weaves various threads together. When the stripping, picking, pressing, carding, and spinning have all taken their toll, an amazing fabric is produced.

Don't misunderstand what I am saying. We are never commanded, or allowed, to do something wrong in order to accomplish something good. It is not because we give in to temptation that we become righteous; rather, because we have been made righteous by Christ's sacrificial atonement we are equipped to overcome temptation.

The sifting is going to come. That's the result of the tragic decisions made in the Garden of Eden. Satan will sift you. But it is always accompanied by a great promise. "Simon, Satan has desired to have you, that he may sift you as wheat. But, I have prayed for you that your faith would not fail. Israel, I am going to allow a sifting season to come, but not one grain shall fall to the ground." Child of God, you are going to be sifted, but you will be saved.

Sifting usually occurs between times of trouble and times of triumph. God will use the sifting to bring you from a place of pain to a place of productivity. He will use it to take you to the next level in your walk with Him. If you are going through a shaking, it's not a breaking, it's a making. God is making something of value out of you. He is working something out of you, separating things you don't need from things you do need. He is turning you into a vessel of honor and glory. He allows the sifting because He loves you. He allows it because He needs you. He has a mission for you to accomplish. Don't forget that.

He sifts you because He desires to use you. When Simon passed through his sifting process he was instructed to reach out to others. The sifting converted him. He would no longer be the same man after the process had done its job. If you will allow God to have His way in your life the change that occurs will be amazing. Peter, who was impetuous and ready to fight for the wrong things at the wrong time, became a man who knew what to do and when to do it.

All of us must be converted in order to be used of God. The old life must be put away. The past must be washed away. Old attitudes must be changed. We cannot move forward until we unload some of the baggage we carry around. Things that are unprofitable must be liquidated. Before David went out to fight Goliath, the Bible says that he "...left his carriage in the hand of the keeper of the carriage, and ran into the army..." (I Samuel 17:22). He could not face the giant while overloaded with cumbersome and unnecessary baggage. Victory belongs to those who not only know how to let go of the past but also know whose hands to put it into.

To be converted means to "turn again." When we get our eyes off the real purpose of life, we need to turn again to the things that matter. When sin rules our hearts, we need to turn again to live an overcoming life. When troubles gain our attention more than God does, we need to turn again to Him. When we forget our purpose, we need to turn again to be reminded of our original calling. When our thinking gets out of sync with God's will, we need to turn again. Conversion is a constant in life.

When conversion takes place, we are reminded that "great obligations follow great blessings." Peter held the keys to unlock the Kingdom of Heaven. It seems he wasn't ready for the task; however, the sifting removed the fickle attitudes from Peter's life. He became one of the most immovable men in all Christian history. He was no longer a man of impulse, but one of insight. His faith was stronger after the sifting, and he accomplished his task.

The strongest people have been shaped by the hardest circumstances. Pearls come from wounds to the oyster. The hurt becomes glorified and valuable as nature encases the offense with a beautiful shell of purity. God wants to turn your adversity into your advantage. He wants to bring healing where the sifting has produced hurting. "Simon, when you are turned again to your purpose, help others."

The power of the Spirit at work in your life wasn't just personal to you, it purposed you, as well. It placed an obligation on your shoulders to reach a world that needs to be converted also.

*Chapter Five*

# Ravaged But Restored

> Fear not, O land; be glad and rejoice: for the Lord will do great things. Be not afraid, ye beasts of the field: for the pastures of the wilderness do spring, for the tree beareth her fruit, the fig tree and the vine do yield their strength. Be glad then, ye children of Zion, and rejoice in the Lord your God: for he hath given you the former rain moderately, and he will cause to come down for you the rain, the former rain, and the latter rain in the first month. And the floors shall be full of wheat, and the vats shall overflow with wine and oil. And I will restore to you the years that the locust hath eaten, the cankerworm, and the caterpillar, and the palmerworm, my great army which I sent among you.
>
> Joel 2:21-25

One thing is for certain: the "Hand of Time" can never be turned back. Once a minute, an hour, or a year is gone, it is gone forever. It is impossible to rewind the clock and start over. We would love to go back to certain times in our lives and relive them. There are people we would hold closer, friends we would cherish more, relationships we would make stronger, if only we could go back. There are opportunities we would embrace, challenges we would welcome, and sacrifices we would make, if given the chance to do it all over again. There are things we would say, apologies we would make, concessions we would give, and forgiveness we would bestow if only we could go back.

There are things we would not say, words we would take back, things said in anger that would forever be erased from our lips, criticisms and unkind things: if only we could go back. If we could roll back time, we'd take more action in some areas of life and less in others. We would make different decisions and take different paths. We would pursue things we once avoided and avoid things we once pursued. We would cherish what we hated and hate what we cherished. But, alas, the sands of time are scattered to the winds of history. They can never be gathered into the hourglass of life again.

Many years ago, a deranged man ran into the Rijks Museum in Amsterdam wielding a knife. He was not looking for a person but rather a painting. His target was a famous Rembrandt called, "Nightwatch." Before anyone could stop him, the man began to slash violently at the painting, slicing it many times. A short time later, another malicious madman ran into St. Peter's Cathedral in Rome with a hammer in his hand. He had no intention of harming people, only a statue. He ran straight to Michelangelo's sculpture, "The Pieta," which depicts the body of Jesus lying on the lap of his mother Mary, and began to swing the hammer with all his might. Before he could be stopped, he caused significant damage to the great artist's most notable sculpture.

Mangled Masterpieces! These works of art were priceless but pummeled, one by a blade, the other with a mallet. Mangled and maligned, they were still masterpieces. Undervalued by one, but greatly valued by others. They were damaged but still divine.

These priceless pieces were not thrown out onto a scrap heap. They were restored. The hands of talented artisans recovered them from their torn, battered condition and made them like new. They were ravaged but restored.

Joel's prophecy rings with hope. "I will restore to you the years that the locust hath eaten, the cankerworm, and the caterpillar, and the palmerworm" (Joel 2:25). Imagine a land fertile enough to support the lives of those willing to work it. Fields are plowed, planted, watered, and well cared for. The seed is specially formulated to yield the greatest harvest. The expectation of a bumper crop is more than mere fantasy. With great patience, the owner of the fields awaits that special day when the wagons are hitched to their horses and made ready to gather in the fruits of his labor. He possesses a pleasant hope and a positive expectation. One by one, the days are marked off the calendar as the harvest draws closer and closer.

Then one day a sound is heard off in the distance. It's a low humming at first, but grows louder with each passing minute. As it does, it becomes more distinct. The old-timers recognize it immediately. They cannot see it yet, but they are fully aware of what is on its way. Watching carefully, they search the horizon, waiting for the ominous proof that their suspicions are true. Pointing to a spot just above a distant treetop, an elder spies what everyone fears. A dark line is forming across the horizon and growing thicker by the second. It is not a thunderstorm or the smoke of a prairie fire they see.

This is an invasion. The invaders are peculiar, yet ferocious. They are not men, but insects. Insects so small you could crush them under your feet without much effort. They are so tiny that a child could scoop one of them up, put it in a jar, and keep it on a shelf without so much as the semblance of a fight from it. These are not individual invaders — these locusts have amassed their numbers. They have banded together and now their numbers reach into the millions.

Alone they are no match for men, but combined they outmatch men altogether. Fortunately, they are not after men. They are after what men need. They are after what men have worked hard for. They want what men desire most. These invaders are hungry. It is a hunger so insatiable that they will devour everything in their path.

The eighth biblical plague upon Egypt was a swarm of locusts. It was so large that no green thing was left standing when the locusts were gone. Standing before this mighty cloud in the sky, the people fear they are facing destruction of apocalyptic proportions. Scientists say that locusts usually live solitary lives. When they leave their solo lifestyle and become a swarming horde, their nature changes.. The color of their skin turns into a shiny black or bright red color. They morph into maniacal creatures whose females begin to lay eggs that hatch in unison throughout the colony. This allows a million locusts to explode into the billions — a force of nature, indeed!

This great army of locusts invaded the land and left no stalk standing. The crops that had been carefully cultivated were gone. The harvest was lost. The fruits of their labor never benefited them. The people were left with nothing. They had been ravaged.

To make matters worse, it seems this had happened more than once. The Bible refers to "the years" that had been devoured. The effect of one, single tragedy has a way of lingering long into the future. Days turn into weeks and weeks into months until you look back and five years have come and gone without any comfort or solace. Joel 1:4 says, "That which the palmerworm hath left hath the locust eaten; and that which the locust hath left hath the cankerworm eaten; and that which the cankerworm hath left hath the caterpillar eaten." It seems you suffer once and an eternal process of loss ensues. First, your heart is broken, then your mind, next your will. The devourers keep on coming until there is nothing left.

If there is one word that best describes the years of many people's lives it would be "wasted." Wasted years are devoured years. Too many people have lived their lives in wasted ways. They have wasted their opportunities, wasted their talents, and wasted their education. They sought after things that proved fruitless. They chased dreams that were nothing more than mirages. Despite their immense potential, they squandered their opportunities.

The locust is a symbol of waste. When he finishes his work, waste is all that remains. All the effort to raise and protect the crop was futile. The locust turned it all to waste.

When some people look at their lives, that's all they can see. Sin has ravaged them leaving nothing but ruin in its path. It has devastated families, killed ministries, and halted progress everywhere it reigns. There are people who look at their relationships and all they see is waste. Sin devoured the good. It choked out the love that once flourished. It robbed them of the joy they once treasured. Sin's nature can seem so docile and singular, but when it gathers its like-minded vices together it morphs into something altogether violent and corruptible.

All of us have wasted things in our past. We have missed opportunities to witness and to work for God. We have wasted blessings that have been bestowed upon us. We have wasted years not fulfilling our callings, burying our talents. We could have done more and achieved more, but the locusts came along and devoured our years. It robbed us of our productivity. It took our strength. It kept us from advancing, from moving in the right direction. We all have locust years.

Locusts come in cycles. In certain parts of the world, locusts swarm in 10 to 15-year cycles. The locusts will rise again, reinforcing their numbers to ravage us once more.

There are many who are like Naomi in the Book of Ruth. The years had been extremely difficult for her. Life had ravaged her family. The cold blast of loss gripped her soul to its very depths. She was dealing with the silent struggle of a life-winter that laid hold upon her spirit. She wanted to change her name to Mara, for she felt that

God had dealt bitterly with her. She needed a little warmth to ease her suffering from the frostbite of bitterness. She was searching, gathering wood for wintery days in hopes of building a little fire within her heart. Her years felt wasted. Her efforts seemed in vain. Her dreams were devoured. She had been ravaged by time. If there is a Naomi reading this, let me tell you that there is hope for you.

Joel said, "You may have been ravaged, but you can be restored." While the past is immutable, restoration remains possible; those lost years cannot be reclaimed, but the value of what was wasted can be renewed. God knows how to make up for what has been lost. He makes all things new. He is a master of restoration. Trust the psalmist when he says, "the Lord restores my soul."

Restoration is a process. It requires stripping off old paint and stains, sanding old edges, and buffing out the scuffs and scars the years have left behind. Heavy use has led to much abuse. Years of ravaging have led to years of unraveling. If God is going to restore you, He is going to put you through a process that may seem painful, but it is always profitable. Unless you are committed to reclaiming what you lost, you will view restoration as impossible. If you will allow Him, He will restore what has been devoured.

Years of ravaging lead to years of restoration. Be patient, you may have been ravaged, but you can still be restored. God wants to do a work in your life. He wants to renew your spirit, redeem your soul, and restore your joy. He wants to give back to you what has been taken from you. You may have lost people you feel you'll never get over, but God can bring new, equally meaninigful people into your life. Missed opportunities allow God to open new doors. Though joy may feel long buried in the depths of depression, God can restore to you the joy of His salvation.

There are people who make their living restoring old things. It is interesting to see what comes in to their shops — an old, childhood toy, a game, a safe, old cars, furniture — all manner of ravaged items. The people who bring them in also want to recover something that was lost in life: something precious. The restoration process reconnects them with things they once loved and cherished. So, the skilled hands of a restorer will take the time to bring it back to life again. The result is always the same — people who thought they would never get that old feeling back are amazed and thrilled because it looks just like new.

Have you ever noticed what people bring into the Church? Old, shattered dreams, unanswered prayers, broken hearts, and cast down spirits; lives ravaged by sin.

Into the House of God they come, and He restores them. The result is always the same — joy, peace, and excitement over the fact that what once seemed lost and wasted is brought back to life again. The House of God is filled with all manner of things that have been ravaged but restored.

## *Chapter Six*

# Plagued But Purposed

> The heavens declare the glory of God; the skies proclaim the work of his hands. Day after day they pour forth speech; night after night they display knowledge. There is no speech or language where their voice is not heard. Their voice goes out into all the earth, their words to the ends of the world.
>
> Psalm 19:1-4

The Psalmist was a stargazer. David seems to have a profoundly deep admiration for the heavens. Perhaps that was due to his unique ability to see and hear what the heavens had to say. Many nights spent under the stars, and many days guiding hungry sheep beside still waters, lent many opportunities to the shepherd king for learning. His education was not astronomy but simple admiration. It was an admiration so deep that it stirred spiritual matters within him and opened his understanding. The sun by day, the moon and stars by night, the radiance of the firmament shouted in proclamation that there was more to this world than what might at first appear.

The Heavens declare the glory of God; the firmament displays his handiwork. Not one day goes by that the heavens do not declare his glory in brilliant eloquence. Not one night passes that isn't illuminated with the message of the universe's Master. The same sun that brightens the United States also brightens Russia. In like fashion, the same moon that gives glory to our night sky gives light to others around the world. The Sun that gives light to the entire Earth represents the Savior who brings the light of salvation to all men. The Moon that shines upon all at night represents the Church that goes into all of the world, penetrating its darkness.

So powerful is the message of the heavens that there is no language that cannot understand what they are saying. If like and unlike languages will listen, they will all hear the same words. If one custom, which varies from another, will pay close attention, they will all see the same splendor. The heavens — the sun, moon, stars, even the skies themselves, have something to say. Their voices echo throughout the earth, their words extend to its four corners.

In every place, these celestial bodies declare something about God. They declare His glory. The word glory here means that which constitutes the honor of God — His wisdom, power, skill, faithfulness, benevolence, as seen in the starry worlds above us, the silent, but solemn movements by day and by night. The idea is that these convey to the mind a true impression of the greatness and majesty of God. The reference here is to these heavens as they appear to the naked eye, and as they are observed by all men. It might be added that the impression is far more solemn and grand when we take into account the discoveries of modern astronomy, and when we look at the heavens, not merely by the naked eye, but through the revelations of the telescope.

It is ironic that while much of science is spent on disproving God's existence, its discoveries most often accomplish the contrary and validate His existence. For some, a casual glance into the sky will bring thoughts of God's omnipotence as they marvel at the stars. But for those who need more proof, we will take a closer look at the largest celestial body in our solar system.

Let's take a trip to Jupiter. It is the fifth planet from the Sun. If Jupiter were hollow, one thousand three-hundred Earths could fit inside. It contains two and a half times the matter of all the other planets combined, and it measures 88,846 miles across its equator. Jupiter is a brilliant celestial body that inspires awe within the attuned heart and mind, but this magnificent creation is not without its own perilous fate. Everything visible on the planet is a cloud. The parallel reddish-brown and white bands, the white ovals, and the Great Red Spot persists over many years despite the intense turbulence visible in the atmosphere. The most energetic features are the small, bright clouds to the left of the Great Red Spot and in similar locations in the northern half of the planet. These clouds grow and disappear over a few days and generate lightning. Streaks form as clouds are sheared apart by Jupiter's intense jet streams that run parallel to the colored bands. Sweeping across the dark band of Jupiter's northern hemisphere is one of the most powerful jet streams in the solar system, driving eastward winds that roar at nearly 480 kilometers (300 miles) per hour. With a diameter more than eleven times that of Earth, Jupiter dwarfs our world so completely that even the "small" storms in this mosaic rival the size of Earth's greatest hurricanes—tempests that would dominate our entire sky. Jupiter is a planet plagued by storms – violent storms, constant storms. The most notable is the Great Red Spot that you will see on just about every image of the planet itself. This boiling blemish is actually a storm that unleashes its rage upon Jupiter. It is a swirling mass of extremely cold temperatures. It is twice as large as the planet Earth. Many speculations have been made as to the depth of this storm. It has a diameter of 15,400 miles, and its winds reach speeds of up to 270 mph. In its entirety, it is one-sixth the diameter of the planet Jupiter, making it the largest storm in the Solar System. Moving counterclockwise, its winds could obliterate an entire town within the space of one minute.

This particular storm has only been visible for the last 300 years. Many experts suggest that it has been brewing for at least 400 years, perhaps even longer. It is only now that science is beginning to understand the significance of this constant storm. Finally, we can hear what the heavens have been trying to declare to us for such a long time.

Depsite the presence of a such a destructive force, it still continues to exist and inspire awe. The storm has left its mark upon the largest planetary body in our Solar System, yet Jupiter continues its orbital path and stays in alignment just as God set it in order long, long ago. The storm has not delayed its destiny. The plague has not paralyzed its purpose.

One thing is certain in life and in much of the world — the weather is going to change. If you don't like the weather around here just wait, it's liable to change in the next few minutes. Predictability is not all that it is cracked up to be. The ability to foreknow and to foresee what a day might bring may not always produce the most profitable outcome. To be sure, only God could handle such knowledge.

If we knew that a storm was going to slam into our life on a certain day, would it change the way we live? It may change us for a day, maybe even a few weeks. Some might live better. Others may live in fear. Paralysis may seize our souls causing us to fail to embrace our joys and miss great moments. Overwhelmed by the magnitude of an impending peril, we would be imprisoned by grief and despair.

For me, it is enough of a burden just knowing that storms are going to come. It is enough for me to recognize that rainy days will arrive and that their clouds will spread out over my life. I fully understand that there will be violent storms that rip things apart and destroy meaningful moments in life. I really prefer not knowing the time and date that they are going to hit. I have received the phone calls that tell of tragedy and loss. My life has been affected by an endless grief that persists beyond any reasonable effort to abort it. Years have a way of easing it, but so far, they have not been able to remove it.

I seem to have reached a place in my life where I am content to know that such storms will come soon enough. Therefore, I will live my life with purpose. Purpose to do my very best and give my utmost. Purpose to love and to be loved, to give and even to receive. Purpose to reach higher and to dig deeper to discover things that were previously unattainable. Purpose to appreciate and hold dear all that is truly valuable in life. Purpose to not get sidetracked with minor issues and miss glorious opportunities to make life better for those I love. Purpose to care, to reach, to pray, to preach, to teach, to learn and to worship. If I must suffer the storms of life, I will suffer with purpose.

Just as our daily activities are planned around a seven-day forecast, in many ways, we plan our lives around an extended forecast, too. Life can be spent questioning the weather. You can mark it down — there are going to be stormy days. There are many storms that assail us. The storms of the not yet, storms of doubt, depression, despair and loss. There will be moments of anguish.

The last few years have been plagued with storms for my family. We lost my 16-year-old niece in a tragic accident. My mother fell and hurt her back. My dad fell and broke his heel, ripping the Achilles tendon loose. My grandmothers were both put in the same hospital on the same day with heart issues. On Easter we got the call that our 21-year-old nephew was suddenly taken from us. Nine years ago, we lost my 46-year-old brother to a heart attack. One year ago, almost to the day of writing this paragraph, I suffered a massive heart attack which has taken me almost an entire year to recover. Just when I thought I was healthy and whole my doctor informed me that I had colon cancer. The old adage rings loudly, "When it rains. It pours!"

Yes, it certainly does. It seems that far too often tragedy is added to trial, and the sum of the two parts is sorrow. An old wound is opened and too many times salt is poured into it. Many are the bitter tears of a man. Many are the afflictions of the righteous. Constant and straining are his storms.

But if we stop to listen, we can hear the voice of the heavens as they declare His glory. If we look upward, we can see the firmament declaring His handiwork. Jupiter has been plagued by a constant storm for over 400 years, yet it has not lost its standing in the universe. The storm has not diminished its capacity, nor rendered it useless. It may not seem valuable to you and me. It doesn't offer any wealth or lend any strength to our economy. What natural resources does it produce for our consumption? It seems to simply be a worthless ball of metal and gas.

Yet the truth is Jupiter plays a major role in the delicate balance of the entire Solar System. If just one planet gets out of its orbital path, mayhem and destruction would ensue upon each of the other planetary bodies. In short, life would cease to exist. It may feel like a stretch to apply such a grand truth to one single life, like mine. But we cannot escape the fact that we do not live to ourselves, and we do not die to ourselves (Romans 14:7).

Storms seem to multiply. Jupiter is plagued by other smaller storms. Some suggest that the Great Red Spot was formed when many small ones merged together. That storm alone is large enough to engulf two earths standing side by side. Sometimes the storms of life multiply by joining forces. They combine their chaos and compound their confusion producing one major catastrophe after another.

No matter what comes our way, we must stay the course that God has destined us to travel. Jupiter remains in its destined pattern despite its storms. That planet, or no other planet, could do that on its own power. The heavens declare God's faithfulness. He faithfully attends to it every day and grants it the fortitude to outlast the blast. God ensures that its strength is greater than the storm.

If you are going through a storm that seems constant, look heavenward. There is a message you need to see written in the firmament. God is faithful, powerful, benevolent, and skillful. The sun shall not smite you by day, nor the moon by night, and neither shall the storm destroy your purpose. We must never give up. Doing so breaks the order of God's plan.

What would happen if you got out of alignment with God's purpose for your life? Jupiter doesn't support life, or does it? Nobody lives on Jupiter. No plant life exists there. No houses or subdivisions are being built there. There are no schools on Jupiter, no thriving industries on its soil. Jupiter is just another mud ball rolling through the universe. It has no real purpose. Or does it? While there may be no actual life on Jupiter, without it the whole universe would be in chaos.

You may not feel that important in the grand scheme of things. It can seem like you're just existing – moving forward without progress, working but not winning, laboring without profit. Storms have a way of lying to us. They tell us we don't matter, that our efforts are pointless. They blind us to our purpose. Storms can make you feel inconsequential, causing you to lose sight of your importance. But they can never erase your God-given significance.

The constancy and consistency of conflict in people's lives can become so overwhelming that they simply give in to the conditions around them and let go. They let go of their will to survive. They let go of their desire to win. They let go of their determination to finish. They let go of their purpose. One thing I learned during my health crisis is that dying is easy – it's living that is hard. To die all you have to do is give in to the force that is drawing you away. But to live you have to make up your mind to withstand it so you can get better. Psalms 118:17 declares, "I shall not die, but live, and declare the works of the Lord." Don't let go.

Before you let life's weather weary you, take a moment and look up. Your purpose is fixed. Your calling is secure. Your importance is intact. The heavens declare it to be so. Someone is counting on you. The operation of the Church depends on you staying in formation. Souls are waiting on you to make up your mind to withstand the weather.

I'm writing to the clap of thunder outside, but I pray there is a flash of lightning-like revelation that illuminates someone's heart today. God is big enough to see you through your storm. He is God enough to see you in your storm. If He knows where you are, you're not lost. Hang in there!

Allow what plagues you to propel you!

*Chapter Seven*

# Persecuted But Not Forsaken

Many a time have they afflicted me from my youth: yet they have not prevailed against me.

Psalm 129:2

It is impossible to peruse the psalms without finding within its passages the perfect image of Christ. The 129th Psalm is no exception. The first impression we get is that the writer is speaking of Jesus.

"Many a time have they afflicted me from my youth, yet they have not prevailed." Herod sought His life the moment Christ was born. Satan stirred his minions to seek the destruction of the savior the moment He entered this world. "The plowers have plowed upon my back: they have made long their furrows" (Ps. 129:3). How true that was of Christ as we see Him praying in the garden full of agony, the furrows of his brow, long and deep. How true it was of Christ at Calvary. On the Cross, thirty-nine stripes upon His back, laid long by the lash, furrowed His flesh deeply. Thus, our first impression is that the text speaks of Christ.

Yet, there is a second impression as well. For we wonder if the author is speaking of himself. The servant is not above his master. The disciple is not above his Lord. Surely, if they afflicted Him, they have also behaved in like manner toward His children. If they have called the Lord of the House Beelzebub, they will call His servants no less. The psalmist declares his own testimony to be that of his master. “They have afflicted me from my youth, yet they have not prevailed against me” (Ps. 129:2). From the moment a child of God is born again, his enemies assail him. Whether it’s his past or some newly introduced adversary, the child of God is pursued from spiritual infancy. It does not take us long to see ourselves in the 129th Psalm. And we must recognize that we will never wear a crown of gold where Christ was compelled to wear a crown of thorns.

In this short psalm, we also see a picture of Israel. From the time they are birthed as a nation there are those who rise up against them. A deeper look within their history reveals how cruelly and craftily their enemies worked to destroy them. Pharaoh forced them to work long hours gathering straw and making bricks. Fearing that a deliverer would arise out of their midst he would drown newborn Hebrew boys in the Nile River. Pharaoh used all his wit and wiles against Israel in an effort to destroy them. The furrows upon their back were long and deep, straight and sadistic. The wilderness was no kinder to them in their youth, either. Even there they had their share of troubles. Bitter waters, serpent bites, and hunger tore at them like a plow digging deep into their collective soul. The Promised Land was not much easier. The land of milk and honey had to be fought for. They were scarcely delivered from the Canaanites when they were challenged by the Philistines, who became their perpetual enemy. Then came the Syrians, the Edomites, and the Moabites. Upon their heels arose the Assyrians and the Babylonians, who ultimately carried them away into captivity.

So we see Christ, His children, and Israel within this psalm. We also see the Church. "From its youth they have afflicted it." Herod sought to kill the Apostles and did, in fact, kill James. The Jews drove the Church from city to city in an effort to destroy its influence. Saul of Tarsus made threats against it and persecuted it like no other had. Pagan religions rose up against the Church. Rome used all of its might to stamp it out, persecuting its participants in unprecedented ways. Thrown to the lions, torn apart by rabid beasts, and sawn asunder by the edge of the sword, the Church was afflicted. In every age, at every stage of its growth, the Church has met with its detractors and defilers. Fires and floods, famine and pestilence, persecution and conquest have each gathered their forces in an effort to prevail against the Church. Even today the Church is under assault.

But mark well my words—against Christ, His people, Israel, or the Church—no matter how long the affliction, its means or method, none of it shall prevail. Christ is greater than any other—no one and nothing shall prevail against Him. Greater is He that is in you than all "they" that are in the world. None shall prevail against you. Israel is the apple of God's eye—none shall prevail against them. Jesus said, "Upon this Rock I will build my Church and the gates of hell shall not prevail against it." The psalmist paints a picture that would inspire Paul to shout, "We are troubled on every side, yet not distressed; we are perplexed, but not in despair. Persecuted, but not forsaken; cast down, but not destroyed" (2 Cor. 4:8-9).

"Many times have they afflicted me from my youth, but they have not prevailed against me!" How often have we heard someone say, "They are against me?" They, they, they…. Who are they? "They said this," "they did that," "they didn't include me," "they don't like me," "they rose up against me." "They" can be anybody or anything. The psalmist had so many tormenters that space did not allow him to name them all. He just put them into one collective "they."

If we took inventory of our foes and afflicters, we could do the same. We have not the time, nor the space to write them all down. It could be a spouse, coworker, employer, friends, acquaintances, even strangers. One translation of the Bible uses the word, "they" 5468 times! The list is too long to mention. Suffice to say, we have to deal with a lot of afflictions from various vendors. Perhaps it wouldn't be such a big deal if we only had to grapple with affliction occasionally, but we wrestle with it often. "Many a time" says the psalmist. Affliction comes in waves, and we wonder if it will ever stop encroaching upon our lives.

Have you ever noticed how cowardly the devil really is? He attacks and afflicts us in our youth. In one sense, it means what it says. The attack is strategically targeted to someone who is newly formed in Christ. But in another sense, it is much broader than that. Youth is a time of weakness. Thus, Satan seeks the weak. We want to tell the devil to pick on someone his own size, but it would do no good. Watch him as he tempts Christ in the wilderness right after His baptism. He thinks himself to be strong and Christ to be weak. He afflicted Jesus in a time of weakness, but he failed to recognize the anointing that was upon His life.

Remember the chapter, "Weak, but Anointed?" You may be wounded, but that doesn't mean you have to be defeated. You may be tired, but you don't have to be trampled on. You may be fatigued, but you need not fear. If you are being persecuted, you can still prevail. It's possible that you are going through things right now that have nothing to do with your salvation. This is not about whether or not you are forgiven or have made mistakes. You are facing them precisely because you are still young in the Lord or because the enemy perceives some weakness within you.

Instead of contending with the enemy, rebuke him in Jesus' name and take hold of your anointing. "Many are the afflictions of the righteous, but the Lord delivers him out of them all" (Ps. 34:19). Reflect upon the scriptural proclamation, "Many times, have they afflicted me, but they have not prevailed against me." Strengthen yourself in this Word. Get a hold of this message and grasp it with all you've got. Christ made it. Israel made it. The Church made it.

You are going to make it!

Sometimes we fight off a lion, only to run into a bear, only to be forced into a fight with a giant. One defeated adversary leads to another. One victory leads to another victory. One triumph leads to another triumph. One mountain climbed inspires us to reach the peak of another. Summits lead to summits. Joy leads to joy. Anointing leads to anointing. The Bible says of our growth in righteousness, that it is like going from "faith to faith" (Rom. 1:17).

We are persecuted, but we are not forsaken. Every test leads to a testimony. Jesus said to His disciples, "They shall lay their hands on you, and persecute you, delivering you up to the synagogues, and into prisons, being brought before kings and rulers for my name's sake. And it shall turn to you for a testimony" (Luke 21:12-13). So, settle it in your hearts … not one hair of your head shall perish … your enemies will not prevail.

In Foxes Book of Martyrs, we read of a woman who was about to die at the stake for her faith. She was expecting a child and began to give birth in her cell. Her cries of agony echoed throughout the prison. Offering her only contempt, the guards derided her, saying, "If you can't bear that which is natural, how can you expect to hold up in the fire?" Through her gasps she replied, "This is the cause of the curse, and I cannot bear it, but that is the cause of Christ, and I can gladly embrace it!" When they burned her at the stake, her test turned into a testimony. Even her enemies noted how well she handled it.

I know what "they" are saying right now. What I am really interested in is what "they" will be saying when your trial is over. They will say, "We did not prevail against them." They will confess, "There is something about him," They will admit, "We could not touch her life." They will testify, "We could not change their course."

Watch Jesus enter the fray of Calvary like a soldier rushing into the dust-cloud of battle. They surrounded Him, but we see Him rise up and cry out, "Father forgive them for "they" know not what "they" do." They put Him in a tomb, but then He arises and shouts, "Go tell them, the promise is unto you and to your children even "they" that afar off." They persecuted Him, but they did not prevail against Him. Instead, He forgave them.

A little forgiveness may be in order today. You may need to forgive more than one person. Maybe – just maybe – you need to forgive yourself too. If you are going to live a prevailing life, forgiveness can't stop with others, it must include you.

I would be remiss if I did not point out that the most agonizing cry upon the cross, for me, was when Jesus cried out, "My God, my God, why hast thou forsaken me?" (Matt. 27:46). Three of the gospels record that Jesus died at the ninth hour of the day. There were two daily sacrifices that took place in the Jewish temple. According to Jewish tradition, the morning sacrifice was at 9 a.m., and the evening sacrifice was at 3 p.m. which coincides with the ninth hour of the day. Twice a day, the shofar would blow, a lamb was sacrificed, reminding the Jewish people of their sin and their need for atonement. At the exact hour that Jesus felt forsaken, those gathered around the cross heard the shofar blowing the Tekiah Gedolah—that long unbroken sound typifying a final appeal to sincere repentance and atonement. When Christ felt forsaken, there rang a certain sound in Jerusalem that reminded mankind that they had not been.

God has not forsaken you. Why don't you let Him turn your test into a testimony?

## *Chapter Eight*

# Little But Loved

> Fear not, little flock; for it is your Father's good pleasure to give you the kingdom.
>
> Luke 12:32

Fear is no respecter of persons—in fact, the most favored people are often tempted to become the most fearful people. I find it ironic that the first words of the angel to the "highly favored" Mary were, "Fear not!" I'll say it again, fear is no respecter of persons. Neither does it pay respect to seasons—it is common in every aspect of life.

To some degree, fear is a good thing. It is a part of our nature that plays a key role in our survival. It is an instinct that kicks into gear when we are presented with dangerous or harmful conditions. Fear is an instinct that tells a child not to touch a hot stove, or to shy away from strangers. Fear is what causes adults to avoid driving under certain road conditions. It is what causes an elderly person to hold a little tighter to the railing when walking up a flight of stairs or to avoid slippery places that might cause a fall. Fear ramps up that part of the brain that initializes our "fight or flight" mentality. In times of disaster or danger, the reaction you see from people, whether for ill or good, is often the result of their fears.

It may sound strange to say it, but there are times when fear is a good thing. But that is not the kind of fear we struggle with. It is not the kind of fear that keeps us up at night or nervous throughout the day. We don't wrestle with that fear which saves us. We wrestle with that fear which enslaves us.

At its core, fear is caused by low self-confidence. It surfaces when we feel unable to handle a situation or circumstance. It rises when we feel incapable of dealing with danger, or feel unable to escape or avoid some trouble, pain, or rejection. When unhealthy fear grips our minds, it is because we feel inadequate to handle what we perceive is happening to us or around us, whether in actuality or only virtually. Such fear incapacitates us and hinders our progress. It stifles our resourcefulness and barricades us behind bars of broken dreams and missed opportunities.

It is imperative that we unmask the mystery of fear and realize the truth about it. Fear is a talented trickster. It wears the mask of deception well. It causes you to believe that what you are afraid of is based in fact, when in reality it is mostly based in fiction. Fear deceives you into thinking you are in danger right now, when in truth, you are only dealing with the idea of "what if this happens to me one day?" or "what might happen in the future?" Fear wants to trick you into running from things that aren't even chasing you. It wants you consumed with the "what if's" in life.

Fear is an emotion. Like all other emotions, it can control you if you allow it. And like all other emotions, it can be changed. Fear is rooted in the threat of loss. Some people fear losing their job or missing out on a promotion. In worst cases, the fear that you will lose your own life to illness - or that you will lose someone you love in a tragedy - can completely envelop your soul. At its deepest level, fear paralyzes and immobilizes us.

Fear is the result of your expectations. The level of expectation you have is often accompanied by an equal amount of fear. The greater your desire for something to happen, the greater the fear of it not happening can be. So, there is often a conflict between what we want to happen and what might actually happen. This struggle always produces fear.

The good news is you don't have to be afraid. Fear does not have the right to demand all your attention. It does not rule upon the throne of your heart. Fear has no authority of its own. It only reigns where it is allowed. When it comes to fear, the experts agree you don't have to be controlled by it. Almost without fail, every counselor will tell you that if you choose to adopt new and empowering beliefs about your fears, they will be easier to overcome.

Take it from the greatest counselor of all: Jesus said, "Fear not." He was talking to people who had everyday worries just like you and me. They had bills to pay, kids to feed, clothes to buy, and roofs to put over their heads. They had relationships to build, opportunities to pursue, and dreams to fulfill. They had governments to worry about, enemies around every corner, and tragedies lurking in the shadows of their lives. Their "rat race" wasn't a whole lot different from ours. Their futures were not much more secure than yours. They often dealt with the "what if's" just like you do. What if we run out of money? What if the kids get sick? What if my health fails? What if I don't survive this? What if my spouse leaves? What if the job doesn't pan out? What if I lose it all? What if God isn't pleased with my life?

Be careful with "what if." It opens the door to "what then." "What then" leads to "why not." She found the perfect husband, why not me? All my friends are succeeding, why not me? They have their dream home, why not me? The "why not" will soon entangle you in knots. It will bind you with the "will nots." I will not try, will not love, will not succeed.

Jesus could see all of that ruminating in their spirits, so He said, "Fear not. It is the Father's good pleasure to give you the Kingdom." Surely a God who is willing to give us a Kingdom will not then allow us to starve on the road to obtaining it. Jesus said, "Don't be of a doubtful mind." If God said He would provide it, then He will provide it. If He promised it, He will perform it.

Something happened to Saul of the Old Testament when he was out searching for his father's wayward donkeys. Samuel met him and anointed him as king of Israel.  After his anointing, Saul never minded those donkeys again. I have seen people waste a lot of their time fretting over insignificant things and misuse their anointing. At the very least, they fail to pursue its purpose in their lives.

We need the anointing. It reminds us that our purpose is greater than our problem. It teaches us that our calling is greater than the chaos that oft surrounds us. It reaches deep into the heart of a man and compels him to seek those things that are above. There are some burdens that the anointing removes from your shoulders, fear is one of them.

We don't have time to be chasing down donkeys. God has called us to something greater. We need to replace the paltry with the purposed. Don't allow your destiny to be compromised by distraction. You're too blessed to be stressed. You're too anointed to be disappointed. It's the Father's good pleasure to give you the Kingdom.

"Fear not, Mary. That which is in you is of the Holy Ghost!" Her greatest source of blessing would also become her greatest opportunity for stressing. Her pain would be the channel for God's purpose to be fulfilled. Her shame would lead to His glory. She would have to stay hidden and kept in secrecy to prevent rumors that questioned her virtue. How could she explain this to anyone? Favor? What favor?

God knew all that, so the angel was commissioned to say, "Fear not."

The Kingdom was born within her. It entered this world through her. Don't fear. God can work in spite of the circumstance. He will accomplish His purpose no matter how difficult it may seem. Don't fear, Mary, your reputation will remain intact — the Holy Ghost is at work in your life.

When you are highly favored you also face the opportunity to be highly fearful. Our low self-confidence will create an attitude of insignificance within us. Mary didn't feel all that special compared to other women. The flock to which Jesus spoke wasn't much to look at. In fact, Jesus called them "little." They weren't many in number. They didn't seem very significant compared to the religious machine of the day. They didn't have the resources or the creativity to stand tall among other institutions of the hour. They were small and insignificant.

Wouldn't it have been easier to accomplish God's purposes through the masses? Wouldn't Christ have been more warmly welcomed had He been born in a palace by a princess? A little girl; likewise, a little flock? It conjures up images of failure and misguided ambitions. It fills the heart with pity. It floods the mind with doubts.

It gets even worse. The original language says Jesus called them a "very little flock." But don't despair because a lack of significance has never hindered God's ability to bless. Someone once reminded us, "Little is still much when God is in it." I hear the prophetic voice of that old man of God, Micah, saying, "But thou, Bethlehem Ephratah, though thou be little among the thousands of Judah, yet out of thee shall he come forth unto me that is to be ruler in Israel; whose goings forth have been from of old, from everlasting" (Micah 5:2). Little flock, little Mary, little Bethlehem, little child of God.

You may be little, but you are loved. Highly fearful? Don't forget, you are also highly favored. You may be very little, but you are greatly loved. Although you feel insignificant, you are special to Him.

Twelve men were no match for a storm. They couldn't bail water fast enough to keep the ship from sinking. They couldn't row fast enough to outrun the downpour. They couldn't swim well enough to survive the treacherous waves. Their ship looked like a tiny dot out on the surface of the ocean. They were too little, very little indeed, to match the might of mother nature. But they were loved, greatly loved. Loved enough that Jesus would defy the very laws of gravity and nature to save them. They were loved so much that He would step into their storm, walk on their waves, override the wind, laugh at the lightning, and thumb His nose at the thunder—just to save them.

One woman was not enough to turn the tide of public opinion in her favor. She crumbled beneath the load of her own sin. She was man-handled through the streets, thrown into the dust, and placed before a crowd of accusers. Who was she to argue her own case? She had been caught red-handed. She was guilty, and that guilt mounted so high that it was about to bury her beneath stones of justice. She could not fend them off. She was too insignificant to fight her own battle; she had too little influence to free herself.

But she was greatly loved. Jesus loved her enough to stoop down to where she was because she couldn't rise to Him. He loved her enough to withstand the Law of Moses and to ignore the demands of her accusers. She was little, but He loved her enough to write in the sand. What did He write? We cannot say with certainty, but what He wrote was enough to turn wrath away and bring mercy to her.

What shall I say of you? You feel insignificant. You feel unnoticed, too little to matter. Fear rises within you when you think about your circumstances. Fear grips your soul when you think about the eventual outcome of your situation. People have forsaken you. You feel overlooked and misunderstood. How many have abandoned you because it seemed you had too little to offer them?

Fear not. You may be little, but you are loved. Christ loved you while you were yet a sinner. He gave His life for you. He loved you enough to fill you with His spirit. He loved you enough to surround you with people who care about you. He loved you enough to keep you safe in a time of trouble. He loved you enough that He would defy the laws of life—He died and rose again—just to redeem you.

He didn't suffer through all of that to let you languish on the road to Heaven. He didn't make promises He never intended to keep. He didn't provide you with things He intends to take back. You may, in fact, be very little compared to so many, but you are greatly loved by One.

If you find yourself in a season of testing, and your heart is troubled, you don't have to be afraid. Take this thought and hold it close daily, "He came that you might have life and that more abundantly" (John 10:10).

Fear may know no season, but neither does favor. You are little, but you are loved. Favor is going to overtake you. The Blessing of Naphtali is upon you. Moses promised the tribe of Naphtali that they would obtain the favor of men and of God. He said they would reap the greatest of benefits because they would be "full of the blessing of the Lord" (Deut. 33:23) They would lack for nothing, possessing both land and sea. In places where footing was sure, they had favor. And, in places where it was not, they had favor. As you read this, I pray that you would walk and live "full of the blessing of the Lord."

## *Chapter Nine*

# Left Behind But Not Left Out

> For who will hearken unto you in this matter? but as his part is that goeth down to the battle, so shall his part be that tarrieth by the stuff: they shall part alike.
>
> I Samuel 30:24

The best of men are men at best. Sometimes the strongest of men can become the weakest of men. The paradox of a man's persona is that he may be known for doing great things and yet be completely incapable of doing anything at all. The rise and fall of someone's level of performance is often the result of situations beyond their control. There are always circumstances and conditions that run contrary to our abilities; times when a runner cannot run, a singer cannot sing, when builders cannot build, or when preachers simply cannot preach. Every man, no matter how strong he is—no matter how accomplished he has become—is subject to forces greater than himself. Sometimes that force is diminished health, lack of opportunity, or fatigue.

Often we are "too faint to follow." We understand the importance of following. We value it as a virtue; a sign of purpose and persistence, of strength and security. All of us want to follow through with what we start. We want to follow the right kind of leadership. We want to follow the Lord. Through the valley or over the mountain—we follow. In joy and in sorrow—we follow. In storm or in sunshine—we follow. There is no wavering within us. Our "want to" is not weakened. The runner wants to run in spite of a pulled muscle. The builder wants to build in spite of the weather. The singer wants to lift his voice even though he is hoarse. The preacher wants to preach even though he is weak.

We want to follow the Lord wherever He may lead us, but the simple truth is that sometimes the way is tough. Sometimes the valley is deep, or the river is swift, and the mountain is high and steep. Often the battle is difficult, and the journey is long and fast paced. Even though we held our own—we kept in step, stayed in stride, and didn't fall out of rank—still we are fatigued. Because of the greatness of the way, we are often pushed beyond the limits of our endurance.

Yes, there are times when we are too faint to follow. We started out with great zeal. We marched with vigor. We began the pursuit with purpose. We worked our plan with passion. We met our enemies with great energy, our foes with fearlessness. We tackled our tasks triumphantly. We maximized every moment and seized the opportunities before us. After all, we knew the Lord was leading us into victory.

But somewhere in the aftermath, our journey zapped us of our strength. And coming down that dusty road, we witnessed things that robbed us of our last ounce of will. In a moment that seemed pregnant with promise, we discovered the stale pallor of defeat. Peril awaited us at the end of the road. Trouble met us in the way. Disappointment delayed our hopes. We beheld what we had longed for, and it was not as we desired it to be. We looked with hope over the horizon to the destination we desired, but it was not as we had imagined. In that moment, our zip and zing were gone. In the absence of the zeal we once felt, we questioned if the journey was even worth it. The energy we had soon became a distant memory. Our will to press on passed on. We felt as if there was no use taking another step. We might as well be honest about it—sometimes the journey takes its toll.

David was divinely ordained as the leader of a band of 600 men whose lives had brought them together. These men had not only heard of David: they believed in Him. They followed him. When they had nowhere to go and no one to go to, they found themselves in the company of Israel's future king. It's a funny thing how the anointing to do, or to be, one thing gets lost in the purpose of something else. And yet that other thing leads directly to the first purpose of your anointing. David was a long way from Israel's throne when he became the captain of a group of discontented, disenfranchised, and indebted men out in the wilderness. Yet, from that woeful and wild backdrop, he would ascend to the greatness of his anointing.

These men chose David, perhaps more than that, he chose them. Once the choice was made, loyalty became their creed. They were loyal to David, and he was loyal to them. When you follow someone, you must understand that you will share in their fortunes. Whether it is good fortune or bad fortune, you will share in whatever fate befalls them. Be it ridicule or reproach, we will bear it if we follow Christ. It may be wonder or woe, but what comes His way will surely come ours.

The good news is that we not only share His misfortune but also the product of it. If we suffer humiliation with Him, then we are assured that we will also share in His glory. If we bear His reproach, we know that we will also reign with Him. If we bear the shame of His cross, we shall also bear the fame of His crown. If anyone of you have made up your mind to follow Him, then decide that you are in it for the long haul. Sink or swim, I will follow him.

These men were all in. And their loyalty was going to be tested. While David and his men were fighting against their enemies, tragedy struck their hometown of Ziklag. The Amalekites invaded the city and burned it to the ground. When David and his men arrived, they witnessed a horrible sight. The city was charred beyond recognition, and their wives and children were carried away as prisoners of war.

Strong men carry strong emotions within. The Bible says David and his men wept until they had no more power to weep. In that moment, the loyalty of those men was put to the test. The Scripture says they spoke of stoning him. They viewed him as the reason this tragedy had taken place. Who could blame them? Their sons and daughters had been carried away. Their wives were gone. Their grief was so great they were not thinking clearly.

But David encouraged himself in the Lord. He sent for the high priest and requested a linen ephod. David sought the Lord in worship and received a Word from God in the midst of tragedy. "Shall I pursue after this troop? Shall I overtake them?" God answered him in the affirmative. "Go after them. You shall overtake them and without fail you shall recover all."

I don't know how they got the word, but the very next verse lets us see that a shift took place in the hearts of those men. Amid unimaginable grief, they heard the Word of the Lord. Instead of stoning David, they stood by him. Instead of taking his life, they put their lives in his hands once again. If you ever find yourself in a place where you are overwhelmed by your circumstances, you are better off if you will trust the man who has heard from God. Sometimes it seems that leaders take us down the wrong path, but if they have a Word from God, we benefit from trusting that Word. Those men were so angry they wanted to kill David. Their truest senses reminded them that there was an anointing upon his life. You can do what you want to do, but I am going to trust the man God has placed in my life. I am convinced he has the Word I need to hear.

David began his pursuit of the Amalekites with all 600 men, but at the Brook Besor things began to break down. Two hundred of these brave fighting men became too faint to follow. They had marched double time from Achish to Ziklag, carrying the same weight all David's soldiers carried. They wept until they had no more ability to weep. They picked up their weapons and packs and left Ziklag with as much zeal as anyone else in David's elite troop. But Besor became their breaking point. They could not take another step. They were so fatigued they could not cross so much as a brook. The Bible said they were left behind at Besor. They were given the task of staying with the stuff. At Besor they stayed with the baggage and kept company with their burdens.

Am I writing to anyone who has ever found themselves at Besor? You reached your breaking point there. You could not go another step. You could not jump a puddle much less fight a battle. At Besor you were surrounded by burdens. At Besor all you could see was the baggage life had left you with. At Besor the world passed you by. Has anyone ever been left behind at Besor? I'm not at all surprised. Besor carries the meaning of coldness. It is a place of the flesh, according to the Hebrews.

David and the remaining 400 hundred men overtook the Amalekites and recovered all that had been taken from them. Each man embraced his wife and children. Each took ownership of his own possessions, making his way back to Besor in jubilation.

But at Besor there was heartbreak and fear. How could those 200 faint and fatigued men face their families? Would they look like cowards? Would they look like weaklings? To the 400 who fought, they seemed unworthy. To them they appeared undeserving. But when the time came to split the spoil they took from the Amalekites, David did what God does for all of us. He said, "What belongs to the man whose strength was great also belongs to the man whose strength was little!"

Besor also carries another meaning of its name. The ancients called it The Place of Glad Tidings. Their grief was about to turn into good news. Much to their surprise, those men discovered that their leader was no respecter of persons. He valued those who stayed with the stuff as much as he valued those who brought more stuff back. Others said, "They don't deserve any of it. They didn't fight for the gold. They didn't risk their lives for the silver. All they deserve is the chance to get their families and possessions back."

But David started handing out the spoils and what he gave to one he gave to all. There is blessing at Besor. You may feel left behind, but you are not left out! God is not going to hold back one blessing just because you are weak. Not because of discouragement or depression, failure or fear. Not because you missed the mark or didn't make the cut. Not because you lacked the talent or the opportunity. Not because of who you are or where you've been. His Word declared that if any man lacked anything He would give it to him.

The anointing is not subject to human weakness—our performance of a task may be affected, but the anointing is still strong. Remember what David said? "I am weak but anointed." The thing that has tried you may have fatigued you, but God did not abandon you. Neither did His blessing. He is still the lifter up of your head, the strength-giver to feeble knees, and the blesser of the stressed. You gave out, but at least you didn't give up. The responsibility you maintain produces the reward you should gain.

You might have been left behind, but you will never be left out.

*Chapter Ten*

# Imperfect But Accepted

> But whatsoever hath a blemish, that shall ye not offer: for it shall not be acceptable for you. And whosoever offereth a sacrifice of peace offerings unto the Lord to accomplish his vow, or a freewill offering in beeves or sheep, it shall be perfect to be accepted; there shall be no blemish therein.
>
> Leviticus 22:20-21

It must have been extremely difficult to please the Lord under the Old Testament Law. Its demands and expectations must have been very difficult to meet. The commands of the Law produced a culture of carefulness among the people of God. By necessity, they were forced to carefully examine every measure of their obedience to the Law in order to fulfill it. Some of its commands were easy to perform—don't touch any dead thing; don't work on the Sabbath, etc. Although many modern Christians consider it irrelevant to us today, much of the Law was filled with minute matters that held deep, significant spiritual meaning. These small details could not be left out. To do so was to incur the anger of God and to reap the judgment of the Law itself.

Upon these little points hung the success or failure of someone's worship and the acceptance of their sacrifices. To be sure, there were many offerings that did not require as much attention to detail. Freewill offerings were not held to the same standard as were the oblations offered for the vows that a man made. Different levels of worship and sacrifice still require different actions. When the Old Testament Jew walked into the sanctuary of old, he had to have the right mindset. He could not be distracted in his worship. His mind had to be completely engaged in what he was doing lest he miss the mark and give his offering in vain. There were rules in place and those rules must be strictly followed. God simply would not accept anything less.

Some, in fact a great many, have suggested that such a Law was too strict. In light of redemption's purpose, it proved in many ways to be just that. But before we totally discredit the Law, let us remember that it was God who designed and implemented it. Under that Law, men did, indeed, draw nearer to God. They found Him to be Holy and discovered that without their own holiness they would never see Him. The Law forced them to think like men who were in the immediate presence of God and to behave themselves accordingly. Their conduct was greatly improved because they had a more vivid awareness of His presence, even if it was His wrath they feared.

The requirements of the Law produced an understanding that God was impartially and immutably holy. It made them recognize that He required man's utmost for His highest. Many churches today have become so seeker sensitive that they have stricken the use of many redemptive words from their vocabulary. Much to my amazement, many of them don't even make reference to the "blood." They act like the people coming out of the world have never seen a movie or been to the doctor before. Who are they kidding? We live in a "blood thirsty" world today. Movies and media, songs and science fiction are full of "blood" references. Yet, these churches have opted out of any reference that might offend or upset their hearers, so they don't talk about the "blood" anymore.

Under the Law, the guilt of sin and the need for atonement vividly reminded the Israelites of one of salvation's most basic tenants. They knew that "without the shedding of blood it is impossible for the remission of sins." If they were to pick a song out of the hymnal and sing it, those old Jews would sing, "What can wash away my sin? Nothing but the blood." They would turn to another page and sing, "Thank God for the Blood."

What would modern church-goers do if they were to have stumbled into that Old Testament Tabernacle and witnessed what the Israelites saw every time they went to church? They would be appalled and aghast at what they saw. Their delicate minds and weak stomachs would not be able to handle the blood spilled out on the floors, splattered upon the altar, and sprinkled on various furnishings within the House of God. How would they have fared in worship in a place where gallons upon gallons of blood were spilled during the ceremonies held there? They can't even handle the word picture of it all. Thank God we don't live under such demands and expectations today. But God forbid that we lose sight and understanding of the blood simply because we are afraid to mention it anymore.

The Law made men realize that salvation could not be obtained without remission of sins and that remission of sins could not be obtained without the shedding of blood. It made men live in respect of the Law itself. Everywhere they went they knew they were under its expectations. This long list of do's and don'ts didn't simply require them to act a certain way at church, it required their conduct to be right everywhere.

Too many Christians only observe the expectations of the Word on Sunday, yet we are to live by them every day of the week. If you live holy on Sunday, live holy on Monday. If you mind the things of the Spirit on Wednesday, mind the things of the Spirit on Thursday. Remember the Sabbath. Keep it Holy. Every day is a Sabbath in the New Testament dispensation—every day is a Holy day. We need to live in a state of conscious awareness that every day we need cleansing and perfecting. God will never demand more of you than He has a right to demand. If He expects something of you, He will empower you to fulfill it.

Without debate, the Law of Moses was a hard taskmaster, and yet it served its purpose well. Throughout its design, we see an image. It is vague at first, hard to really visualize, but it is there, nonetheless. As we stare into it, the image becomes more and more clear to us. Then, in a moment of revelation, we see through the demands and requirements, we look through the blood and the loss of life and we see a man. Our intense observation brings us a divine revelation. It is no longer the Law we see, but we see the Lord. For the Law was a schoolmaster to bring us to Christ. I had many teachers in school, few of whom I thought were easy to get along with or to understand. Many of them were demanding and, to me, a little unfair. Some were not kind at all. One or two of them even failed me. But as I matured, as I learned, I began to understand a powerful truth. Through them I saw my education. I gained knowledge and understanding. I realized they demanded so much because they had so much to give.

That's how God was under the Law—demanding. He was so demanding because He had so much to give. If we peer long enough through the blood-stained lens of the Law, we see our salvation. We see our Savior.

Thus, we find the Gospel in the Law and the Law in the Gospel. Jesus said, "I did not come to abolish the Law. I came to fulfill it." He came to achieve what no man had been able to accomplish, meeting the demands and expectations of the Law. His objective was to be to us and for us what the Law could not be, so that through His fulfillment we might be saved.

Jesus Christ became our sacrifice. The High Priest entered into the Holiest of Holies once a year to offer the blood of a sacrifice. This was a yearly requirement for their atonement. Christ entered into that Holy Place just once, not by the blood of a bull or a goat, but by

His own blood. This He did just once for His sacrifice satisfied the demands of the Law. In that Holy Place, Jesus obtained redemption for us all.

Writing to the Hebrews, Paul said, "For if the blood of bulls and of goats, and the ashes of an heifer sprinkling the unclean, sanctifieth to the purifying of the flesh. How much more shall the blood of Christ, who through the eternal Spirit offered himself without spot to God, purge your conscience from dead works to serve the living God?" (Hebrews 9:13-14).

The Levitical writer said of the sacrifice, "It must be perfect to be accepted." That haunts me for many reasons. My righteousness is as filthy rags. "There is no good thing that dwells in us," Paul said. We were born in sin and formed in iniquity. None of us would have been a sufficient sacrifice. Not one of us could have paid the price in full. "It must be perfect to be accepted."

That cut us right out of the equation. Our natures are tainted. We are filled with spots and blemishes. We are full of defects and distinct sins. We have operated out of impure motives and have been given to unrighteous ways. All of us have sinned and fallen short of the glory of God. The Law would never have accepted us. We would be most miserable if we had to live up to its expectations. We could never be perfect; therefore, we could never be accepted.

But let us not despair. Jesus Christ is perfect. He passes every inspection and fails not to meet the measure of the Law's demands. His nature is perfect. Nothing about His birth stained His character. He was tempted in all points just as we are, yet He never sinned. Even when Satan himself came to inspect Christ, he found nothing evil or vile within Him (John 14:30 KJV). He was without spot or wrinkle or any such thing. His motives were always pure. He did nothing of Himself, for His own cause. There is no trace of evil ambition within Him. He was not sinister, sordid or selfish in any of His ways. His deeds were honest, and His integrity was intact. That is why Pilate could find no fault with Him.

His spirit was right. His motive was love. Everything He did flowed out of the current of unconditional love for humanity. He lived a life of obedience. His relationships were in order. His perspective was never out of sync with Heaven. He offered Himself as a perfect sacrifice. He gave His body to be tortured and His mind to be crushed and broken, even unto the agony of death. He gave Himself for us, a perfect Sacrifice. All that the Law could ask was in Him. Stretch the measure to its utmost length and still Christ goes beyond. He exceeded the demands of the Law. It must be perfect to be accepted and so it was. Christ was perfect.

Do you realize what that means for us? It means that we can be saved. It means that we can be forgiven. It means we can rest in the sacrifice of Christ. We can take advantage of His perfection. When we come to God, we don't have to stand before Him in fear of rejection. We can stand within the shadow of His sacrifice. We are covered by the blood of Christ. We are redeemed by His death.

Imperfect people can stand in perfection before Him. Hebrews 10 explains this in depth: "The Law could never perfect its participants." It was impossible for the blood of bulls and goats to take away sin. The priests gave daily offerings and sacrifices that couldn't save anyone. Their practices were perpetual, even redundant. But Jesus gave one offering, and by that one offering, perfected them that are sanctified. The Law made nothing perfect. However, Paul spoke about a better hope that did. That "better hope" was Jesus.

If you need salvation, all you must do is hide beneath the power of His sacrifice. Repent of your sins. Submit yourself to His death through baptism. Hide behind His goodness. Be filled with His Spirit!

You are imperfect, but you can be accepted!

*Chapter Eleven*

# Faint But Not Faint-Hearted

And Gideon came to Jordan, and passed over, he, and the three hundred men that were with him, faint, yet pursuing them. And he said unto the men of Succoth, Give, I pray you, loaves of bread unto the people that follow me; for they be faint, and I am pursuing after Zebah and Zalmunna, kings of Midian.

Judges 8:4-5

"I'm a little tired. I'm a little weary. I'm a little wounded. I will lay me down to bleed for a while and then get up to fight again!" These were the words of an unnamed soldier during a battle that has long since been forgotten. They are the words of a man who was "Faint, But Not Faint-Hearted."

Gideon had been heralded as a mighty man of valor and was called upon to deliver Israel from the oppression of the Midianites. For seven long years the hand of Midian prevailed against Israel. The tyranny was so terrible; its strength was so severe that Israel was forced to dwell in caves and dens, strongholds, and fortresses wherever they could find them. Israel would sow their crops in secrecy trying to avoid detection by the greedy Midianites who would steal their harvest from them. When it looked as if they were actually going to gather the harvest for themselves, the Midianites would join forces with the Amalekites and the children of the east and plunder Israel's harvest. This mighty Midianite "Axis of Evil" encamped against them and destroyed the increase of the earth. There was simply nothing Israel could do. The sheer number of invaders covered the landscape like a swarm of grasshoppers. Their camels and cattle were innumerable as were their chariots and their pillagers.

Greatly impoverished, all Israel could do was cry out to God. In their trouble, He heard them. The Lord sent them a prophet and a promise. Deliverance was on its way! An angel was dispatched to a winepress where Gideon was threshing wheat in an attempt to hide it from the Midianites. The Lord spoke to Gideon saying, "Surely I will be with thee, and thou shalt smite the Midianites as one man."

After much deliberation and confirmation that he was in the will of God, Gideon amassed an army of 32,000 Israelites. He leads them to the well of Harod, just to the south of the Midianite encampment. The combined forces of the Midianites and the Amalekites were as innumerable as the sands of the sea. Gideon probably thought his army stood little chance against such a mighty force. Imagine his surprise when the Lord said, "You've got too many men to fight with!" If Gideon thought he stood little chance with 32,000 men, he was not alone. When given the chance to back out of the fight, 22,000 of them went back to their caves. With only 10,000 left the Lord said, "There are still too many to fight with." God proceeded to whittle this ragtag army down to just 300 men!

The odds were not in their favor. How could so few do so much? How could such a small force possibly intimidate, much less defeat, an innumerable host? Let us never be too quick to assume that a little in God's hands is the same as a little in ours. Dividing that group into three companies, Gideon armed them with trumpets and lanterns covered with something to hide the light—the Bible calls them pitchers. At the appointed time, they blew the trumpets, broke the pitchers, and cried out, "The sword of the Lord and of Gideon!" The Midianite host was so scared they started killing one another and running away from the battle.

It is while Gideon's small army is chasing after them that we find a compelling statement within our text. These 300 men were not cowards. They were not unwise warriors. When given the chance to back down, they stayed. When given a chance to quench their thirst, they did so with a watchful eye. When given the command to charge, they rushed toward the enemy camp with little more in their hands than broken pieces of pottery and a trumpet.

When the enemy retreated, they chased them even though they were physically exhausted. The fight had taken their strength from them, but their lack of strength had not taken the fight out of them. To the men of Ephraim Gideon said, "We are faint, yet pursuing!" At Succoth, Gideon asked for bread to strengthen his men so they could continue the battle and win total victory. They were "faint, but not faint-hearted."

I realize that many of you are engaged in a battle of your own. I am writing to people upon whom the battle has taken its toll. It's taken your strength, but it hasn't taken your fight. You are faint, but not faint-hearted. I have a little bread for you today, a little nourishment, a little reviving and renewal.

When we see men who are faint, we need not rush into judgment about their lack of strength. It may be that their weariness has proven something about their character. It might just be an indicator of the kind of stuff they are made of. Having done all to stand, they keep standing. Having gone as far as flesh and blood can possibly take them, they are faint, but not faint-hearted. They are perplexed, but not in despair, persecuted but not forsaken, troubled but not in distress. They may look defeated, but they are really victorious. They might appear to falter, but they are really rising up. When you see someone that appears to have been through it, don't rush to some rash conclusion about their spiritual mindset and think they won't make it. I have a feeling their testimony is, "I am faint, yet pursuing."

The best of men are men at best. In our flesh, we can do nothing of any spiritual significance. Paul said, "In me, that is in my flesh, dwelleth no good thing." Human nature is inferior to the Spirit. Not only is it filled with evil ideas and pursuits, it is weak, very weak. It doesn't take a whole lot to make us tired. It doesn't seem to require a tremendous amount of effort to weary the flesh. The least amount of labor or exercise seems to drain our energies. Some people get tired just tying their shoes! The simplest thought processes can weary some people. The easiest job can take its toll on our flesh. It doesn't mean that we are lazy and lethargic or that we don't possess any mental stamina. It just means that anything that challenges our flesh can be a great task for it to accomplish.

That's because the flesh wants to be at ease. It wants comfort and luxury; moreover, it wants to be coddled and looked after. It doesn't want to be stretched, challenged, or constrained in any way. The carnal mind is enmity with God, and when you start forcing your mind to think and to act like Christ, it will war against you. Just lose one night's sleep and you will see just how feeble your mind really is. Your fleshly nature will fatigue faster than you can renew it. That is just a human condition.

Gideon and his men were faint because they had been up all night. They hadn't had any sleep. They were not well rested. Their minds weren't as clear and sharp as they should have been - their muscles began to resist any movement at all.

We may carry out in the spirit what we are too tired to do in the flesh, but we will never accomplish in the flesh what we are too weary to do in the spirit. Indeed, the spirit is willing, but the flesh is weak. We need to learn to sit at His feet and learn of Him. Jesus would have Martha care about her guests and serve them graciously, but not at the expense of being encumbered with too much. There comes a time when we have to sit down and renew our strength. You can work hard for all the right things and right reasons only to find yourself completely drained of all mental and spiritual strength. In those moments, you find yourself faint, but not fainthearted. You desire to keep working even though you are exhausted.

Listen, it is possible to attempt too much and accomplish next to nothing simply because you lack the strength to do anything very well. What one rested, renewed man might accomplish with one blow, has more impact than many feeble strokes where one's energies are depleted. We need to learn this lesson because we are on the go all the time. We never stop or take a break. We never relax, sit down, and just let God renew our strength. Even Jesus withdrew a little way off from the expectations placed upon Him. Even when circumstances seemed to oppose rest, we find Him asleep in the hinder part of a ship during a storm.

Make no mistake about it, "They that wait upon the Lord shall renew their strength." Just because individuals are not busy doesn't mean they aren't taking care of business. Jesus is the Bread of Life. He is the bread offered at Succoth, which renews men for the fight.

The stress and strain of the battle had taken its toll on those men. Has there ever been an hour when you have felt more stress in your life than right now? Has there ever been a time when you have felt strained like you feel it right now? The pressure is on. Life doesn't seem to be getting any easier. It's not letting up for most of us. Not a few of God's people are operating under circumstances that seem to require superhuman strength.

Some instances of faith are not for the faint of heart. Mustard seed faith may move mountains, but many times we face entire mountain ranges that must be removed. Every-day, ordinary faith is nothing to be scoffed at, but we are facing times that require the faith of the very elect. We are modern day patriarchs and matriarchs of the faith once delivered to the saints. These are extremely trying times. They are times of great testing and trial. We cannot afford to allow the things that weary our flesh to also weary our hearts.

Just because you are weary doesn't make you a failure. These men had been very successful. Three hundred of them had put to flight an army of 150,000 plus. I've heard people say, "Working for God is easy. It's refreshing. It's energizing." (Those people have never operated a youth camp.) In many ways that is true, but it is also very likely to sap you of your strength, as well. If you are tired in your labors for Christ, don't be discouraged. You are not a failure just because you feel faint. Many have grown discouraged because of the greatness of the way and the strength required to walk it, but blessed are they that endure to end. They are not failures. They are successes.

Gideon's men were faint, but they were not faint-hearted. They suffered loss but refused to lose. Their will was weakened, but not broken. They were a little depleted, but would not live defeated. They were "faint yet pursuing." Unable to march fast or ferociously, they determined to continue marching. Too feeble to strike their enemy with fury but strike him they did.

Once engaged in battle, they were resolute in their pursuit of victory. Driven by a firm belief, they did not waver in wanting to conquer Midian. They did not cower behind their weaknesses. There was no intention to turn back at this point. They were faint, but they were in pursuit. Every one of them was determined to go forward.

These men refused to rest on their accomplishments or hand the battle over to other troops. They didn't say, "We've done our part. Now let someone else do theirs." They made up their mind to see the battle through. They were driven by hope and there is nothing more compelling than that. They had hope that victory would return prosperity and peace to their land, their families, and to their loved ones. Hope that victory would bring salvation and restoration. They had hope that winning the war would return them to their homes and villages – that it would get them out of the caves and dens. Hope gave them a promise that they could come out of hiding and remove the shame it brought upon them.

Hope prevents surrender. Hope will carry you past weakness and fear. It turns the possibility of quitting into the certainty of persevering. Tired? Feel like you are going under? Ashamed and embarrassed? Have you isolated yourself? Don't lose hope! Hope fuels your future. It ensures that you keep moving forward.

Too many people give up when it feels like they cannot accomplish in the flesh what they started in the spirit. We've got to learn to serve the Lord no matter how we feel. We need to serve Him even if every movement and every step is painful. Sometimes you have to press through the pain. You have to lift one more burden even though it feels as if it will break your back. You must carry your cross even though you know its leading you to a crucifixion. You have to walk one more mile even though you don't feel like taking one more step. Serve Him when you feel like anything but a servant.

We cannot afford to become faint-hearted. We must be courageous when we feel no encouragement. We must be hopeful when we feel hopeless. We must pursue the prize when we see no prize to pursue. Be not weary in well doing. Reaping season is right around the corner.

It's okay to be faint, just don't grow faint-hearted. The victory is just around the next bend. What started for Gideon in the middle of the night was over before the sun came up in the morning. "Weeping may endure for the night, but joy is coming in the morning!" (Ps. 30:5).

*Chapter Twelve*

# Delayed But Not Denied

> I will stand upon my watch, and set me upon the tower, and will watch to see what he will say unto me, and what I shall answer when I am reproved. And the LORD answered me, and said, "Write the vision, and make it plain upon tables, that he may run that readeth it. For the vision is yet for an appointed time, but at the end it shall speak, and not lie: though it tarry, wait for it; because it will surely come, it will not tarry.
>
> Habbakuk 2:1-3

It is not the wanting of things that is difficult; rather, it is the waiting on them that creates distress. We humans are those odd creatures who have little patience to wait for what we desperately want. It is this very flaw in our nature that creates the need for seasons in our lives. When it is freezing outside, we can hardly wait for summer to thaw us out. When the mercury boils to sizzling summertime temperatures, we can hardly wait for winter's blast to cool us off again. Seasons bring change. They keep us from getting too comfortable or uncomfortable with life. Seasons bring growth, and they also bring certain death.

In life, we will always have seasons of struggle and testing. There are going to be times when everything we do will seem to turn out all wrong. Regardless of our prayers and consecration, adversity will always arise. We need to understand that seasons are set. They are predestined to run their course; allotted a certain and determined beginning and conclusion. Spring starts in late March; Summer begins in late June. Fall begins in late September, and winter doesn't really start until just a few days before Christmas.

Just as we cannot force earthly seasons to arrive or to pass, likewise, we cannot simply pray away God's seasons. We need to learn this valuable lesson: "The season is set." In spite of our dislike of the icy grip and the chilling winds, we need to learn to trust God to stay on schedule. Solomon said, "To every thing there is a season, and a time to every purpose under the heaven." Every season has its purpose. Without going into detail, we understand what that means. Tulips don't grow in the cold; they need a winter dormancy to develop roots. Tree pollen doesn't fill the air in the summertime. God has a purpose in not allowing us to be fruitful all the time. One season brings the planting of the seed and another brings the harvesting of it. No matter what you do, you cannot change that.

I have decided that some things are not meant to be changed but rather survived. If you can't alter it, then make up your mind to outlive it. If your life is like a tree planted by rivers of living water, then be like a tree. In the frosty arms of winter, the forest silently refurbishes its strength, preparing for its next season of fruitfulness. Its branches, beaten by wintry blasts and laid bare, offer no comfort to anyone. Yet the tree is as much alive as it ever was. Its sap and substance have gone underground, deeper into the soil of its planting. Its roots cling tightly to the soil. When springtime rolls around it will push its way back to the surface and bud in a brilliant fashion. If we are ever going to experience genuine renewal, we must make up our mind to outlast the blast.

Temporary setbacks create opportunities for renewal and the

refreshing of our commitment. Success is seasonal, but so is failure. Laughter is seasonal and so is sorrow. Sunshine is replaced with rain, and rain is replaced with sunshine: on and on the cycle goes. Whether it's raining, or the sun is shining, hot or cold, don't forget that every phase of your life has its own purpose.

We want the sunshine, but we must wait out the rain, so teach us, Lord, to sit back and glean from the storm. We often make the mistake of making permanent decisions based on temporary circumstances. Someone said, "Patience is a tree whose root is bitter, but its fruit is sweet." The reward of patience is not having to gradually amend your amendments. Patience teaches us that temporary circumstances do not always require immediate action. Some fires are not self-sufficient enough to perpetuate themselves and will soon burn out. They do not require the aid of the local fire station. They only require a little watching, a little patience. Every storm runs out of rain.

That's what James meant when he said, "Let patience have her perfect work" (James 1:4). Patience results from trust. I have discovered that prayer brings us patience. You can't trust a God you don't talk with. Prayer is the seasoning of good judgment. It is the difference maker between us constantly running around putting out little fires and focusing on the raging inferno that needs the most attention. In our relationship with God, we need to be patient with the process that brings about our purpose. All of us have an appointment with destiny. God has a plan for all of our lives. To each of us God has a chosen vision, and for us collectively God has a chosen vision. A vision for His Church and a vision for each of his children. That plan is to bring us to a place of spiritual prosperity and blessing.

We need to understand something about God—He is a God of order. He does everything by appointment. He has set a predetermined appointment to bring to pass His promise in our lives. We read these words 497 times in the Bible, "It came to pass." Ultimately, everything we go through comes to pass; it doesn't come to stay. It comes to pass in order to bring us to our destined appointment, reminding us that He has already made a way of escape. It comes to pass to make us realize that in spite of all the temporary chaos, there is a destined deliverance. It comes to pass so that we understand we don't have to stay the way we are, so we can enjoy living again. It comes to pass to make us realize that nothing the enemy can do to us can abort the plan God has for us. Remember this so you won't be tempted to rush God's timing and order of things. God explained to Habbakuk, "The vision is for an appointed time. So don't be discouraged when you don't see results right away. Just patiently wait for it. Even if it the odds are stacked against it, it will come to pass, and it will be right on time. It may be delayed, but it is not denied."

When God speaks a word into our lives it is like a seed; it takes time for it to sprout. God knows when we have reached the time of our germination. When I was a kid, we did one of those experiments in school where you place a seed in some soil inside of a little cup. We set them on the ledge of the window in the classroom, and every day we would check to see if the seed had produced anything. During those few days we had to trust the unseen process that promised its growth. Finally, one morning we could see a green stem stretching upward from the soil. The experiment worked.

We need to learn to put our trust in the seed that God plants into our lives. When the promise is grown in the fertile soil of a faith-filled heart and reaches the time of maturation, it will come to pass. It won't be by might, nor by power, but by the supernatural Spirit of the Living God. I feel like David—"My times are in His hands." My appointment is predetermined. There is peace in knowing that God has included us in His plan, even if we don't have all the details. He will finish the work He started.

Somewhere in the recesses of our mind there should be an inner knowing that directs us toward an expected end. It is that kind of awareness that will enable us to get out of bed in the morning and keep fighting for survival. We need to be the kind of people who can look the enemy in the eye and say, "My life cannot come to an end until certain things have come to pass. It's not over until God says it's over." How can we say that? It is because we have this inner knowing, too deep to be explained, but it is just as real as the sun in the sky. It is a knowing that tells us, "Even if the circumstances contradict the purpose of God in our lives, the purpose will always prevail." Jesus' experience at Calvary seemed to contradict the purpose of His ministry, but He could face it with certainty knowing that His purpose would prevail. He said, "For this cause came I into the world and to this end was I born."

There is probably a parent reading this whose child is veering away from his or her destiny. You trained them and brought them up in the way they should go. Despite your efforts, they are straying further away from it. Their return may seem impossible, but God knows how to make all things work together for good to them that love the Lord. As parents we should strive to give our kids a sense of destiny. They need to know they have immeasurable potential. If they ever grasp that, nothing will stop them. To be sure, they are likely to deviate from the path on occasion, but at least they have one to travel. Far too many children today don't even know what the path looks like. That's why I believe kids should have a strong sense of direction. An aimless generation is the result of parents that have lost their aim.

In Genesis, the Lord promised Eve a seed. It would conquer the serpent and bring salvation to humanity. Eve had two sons whom she thought would be the sons of promise. As it turns out, they weren't. The eldest viciously murdered the youngest and became a fugitive on the run. Her destiny seemed invalidated, but the purpose always prevails.

God unwrapped the blanket of failure from around her and blessed her with another son. She named him Seth. Seth means, "substituted." It comes from a Hebrew word which means "to appoint" or "place." Holding that baby in her arms, she realized that if God appoints a thing, it will come to pass. It doesn't mean the enemy won't try to stop it or even appear to succeed at nullifying it. But, if God said it, you can rest assured. It may be delayed, but it can never be denied.

God's purpose was not aborted when Cain killed Abel. In spite of the fact that life has its broken places, ultimately everything God says will come to pass. For He Who has begun a good work in us will perform it. One writer said, "He will perfect that which concerns me." If you have experienced loss, God has a way of restoring things you thought you would never see again. Eve held that little baby boy in her arms and shouted, "God hath appointed me another seed instead of Abel." The promise was delayed but not denied.

The real test of faith is in facing the silence of being on hold. If you have ever tried to get a call through to a business, you know what being placed on hold is like. Suspended times of silence can be extremely exasperating. In fact, you get to thinking that—no matter how many times the automated voice reassures you that help is on the way—you have been forgotten about. These people are masters at taunting you while they make you wait. Short pauses in the music just to make you think someone is picking up the line. A soothing voice constantly consoling you with the promise that your call will be answered by the next available representative. You know what I'm talking about. I was on hold the other day for about ten minutes. Finally, the automated voice asked me to leave a message and they would call me back. When they do call me back, I'm going to put them on hold!

Your patience will get a workout when God's answer is silence. When you call and call only to be put on hold, you need to remember that God takes calls in order too. He synchronizes His answers to accomplish His purpose. God is not easily spooked by what we call an emergency.

He always remembers the "Noahs" riding out the deluges of life. God knows where you are and what you are facing. God remembered

Noah and all the wild animals and livestock that were with him in the ark, and He sent a wind over the earth and the waters receded; likewise, He remembers you. Your flood may be prolonged and agonizing, but God will always remember His purpose for your life. When He does, His spirit will drive the flood waters back. Your answer may be delayed, but it is not denied.

Regardless of the obstacle in your life, there is a wind of God that can drive the enemy out, the floodwaters back, and the adversity away. For every mighty problem, there is a mighty rushing wind. If you are waiting at your own personal Jerusalem to be endued with power from on high, tarry as long as it takes for the wind to arrive. The promise, the purpose, and the appointment may be delayed, but it is not denied.

## *Chapter Thirteen*

# Bruised But Not Broken

> For the fitches are not threshed with a threshing instrument, neither is a cart wheel turned about upon the cummin; but the fitches are beaten out with a staff, and the cummin with a rod. Bread corn is bruised; because he will not ever be threshing it, nor break it with the wheel of his cart, nor bruise it with his horsemen.
>
> Isaiah 28:27-28

The art of husbandry was taught to man by God; thus, Isaiah says, "His God doth instruct him to discretion and doth teach him." Having been sent from the Garden of Eden, Adam would need more than a little instruction in survival, so it seems that God gave him an elementary introduction to the art of sowing and reaping.

In Eden, the earth produced after its own kind. Adam's primary concern in the garden was to tend it. A mist came up from out of the earth to water the garden. Plants simply reproduced fruit according to their divine design. Everything Adam needed was provided for him at no real expense. Only after the fall of man do we hear the Lord pronounce the judgment of labor upon Adam. His grain will be gathered by the sweat of his face and only through hard work will he eat.

So, God taught man how to farm. He would plow all day long just to sow seed into the ground. His labor produced hope, therefore the husbandman plowed in hope, and he sowed in hope. The busting of the sod is necessary for the production of the grain. The husbandman is taught discretion in his sowing. He knows what ground receives what grain best. There is no wasting of his time and no haphazardness to his reaping. Carefully, God instructed man concerning the manner in which seed is chosen, ground is tilled, and harvests are reaped. But He has also ordered the process that brings the grain from the field to the table.

Ancient farmers did not have the benefit of modern machinery. They used simple crude instruments to thresh out the various grains they gathered. Yet, they were extremely wise and ingenious in their operations. Sometimes a heavy object was dragged over the corn to tear out the grain. It is what Isaiah meant when he spoke of the "threshing instrument." When that instrument did not work, they would employ the use of the heavy wheel of a cart. This they would roll back and forth over the grain. For smaller grains like dill and cumin, they would use a simple staff or slender switch.

So, the Bible says they did not roll the cart's wheel over the fitches or the cumin but only over the weightier grains. Even in doing that, they were very careful not to crush the bread grain. In the threshing, the bread grain is only bruised.

There is another "threshing instrument" used in Scripture that we often overlook, although we read of it many times. It was known as the "tribulum." This was a "threshing board" about three to four feet wide, six feet long, and consisting of two or three wooden planks assembled to one another. On the underside of these narrow boards, several cutting flints were securely fitted. Some models had holes hollowed out, and rocks were placed tightly into them. The tribulum was pulled over grains in an effort to separate them from the stalks they once clung to for life.

The ancient threshing tool gave rise to the Latin word tribulātiō, meaning "affliction." From this imagery of pressure and separation, we get our modern word "tribulation." This word was used as an instrument to convey a greater truth concerning the children of God. Tribulation became synonymous with other words like sorrow, distress and adversity. These are the appointed means for the separating in men of whatever in them is light, trivial, and unprofitable. These are they, which separate the chaff from the wheat. The writers called these sorrows and trials, "tribulations"—threshings of the inner man, without which there could be no fitting him for the Kingdom of God. It is not a strange statement at all, when we hear the disciples say, "We must through much tribulation enter into the Kingdom of God."

Different seeds have different needs. Some thrive in places that others could not survive. Some need a lot of water and some need very little. Some seeds need sunshine and others need shade. Some seeds need warm climates and some cling to cold. Certain seeds do well in clay and some in sand.

The point is that the husbandman uses wisdom and discretion in planting his crops. But he also uses discretion in harvesting them. Some grains are heavy and need a fair bit more threshing. Heavier instruments are required to get the best out of those crops. On the other hand, some plants are smaller and more tender, and they require only a little threshing to separate the chaff. So the farmer employs lesser machinery for them.

Like grains, not all of us are the same. Because of our differences, God often chooses between what seems fair and what is fitting. We want to grow where we want to grow. We want the sunshine when we would thrive better in the shade. We want the warm climate when the truth is we are better off in the cold. We want the clay when we would produce much more in the sand. God uses discretion in sowing our lives.

He also uses discretion in reaping. He doesn't thresh us all the same way. Just as He has taught the husbandman to distinguish between the grains, He employs the same wisdom when it comes to you and me. Different sorts of men require different sorts of threshing. He does not try us all alike. We do not all pass through the same agonies, nor are we all threshed with the same terrors and trials. One escapes with only being beaten with a rod, while another feels the heavy hooves of horses upon his soul. Threshing is common to all men, but it is always done with discretion, and it will not last forever.

"Simon, Simon! Satan hath desired to have you that he may sift you as wheat." Even the best of us still have a little chaff somewhere in our lives. Being men, we are not perfect and are still plagued with the infirmity of our humanity. There are things in our lives that were necessary to us at one time or another, but they no longer profit us. The wheat was once joined to the straw. The straw sustained it and supplied it with nourishment. But when the wheat is harvested, the straw serves no good purpose. It must be separated. The husk remains after the harvesting, and it, too, must be removed.

Even among the holiest of lives there is something that must be separated. It may be an evil imagination, an impure motive or agenda, but it must be removed. There is still something of this world that we cling to that must be let go of. So, the threshing comes to separate us from our earthly connections. Spurgeon said, "What is bred in the bone is hard to get out of the flesh." Therefore, the hand of God wisely applies the threshing instrument to our lives in order to separate us from things that are not profitable.

The sifting process is the very last process of the harvest. Because the threshing floor was usually just a flat spot on the ground, rocks would often mingle with the grain. The winnowing fan tossed the wheat into the air so the wind could blow the chaff away. However, the heavier bits of stone mixed in with the grain would fall straight back to the ground along with the wheat. For this reason, a sieve was then used to sift the mixture and separate the stones from the good grain.This last process perfected the harvest.

God used Satan as a sifting instrument in Simon Peter's life. There were pieces of earth still clinging to his soul, and they needed to be removed before he could become the voice of God. The Lord allowed him to be sifted so that he could be saved. If you're going through the sifting process, then be of good courage the tribulum has already passed through this part of your life.

God's threshing is done with great discretion. The fitches, a small seed used for flavoring cakes, was not crushed under the weight of the massive wheel. The cumin was not ground to pulp by the heavy wheel either. They were removed from the stalks by being beaten out with a staff. The fitches and the cumin had need of nothing more than the touch of a rod. For tender seeds, the farmer used gentle means, and for the harder grains, he reserved the sterner processes.

Our threshing is in God's hands. "Whom the Lord loveth He also chasteneth." No other but God could exercise such discretion in threshing the lives of men. If it were left up to us, we might use the wheel when only the rod is necessary. We might employ the staff where the drag is needed. We ask for trouble when we try to do the threshing ourselves. We would grind tender plants to powder. So let us be wise and discreet and leave the process to the One whose wisdom is supreme.

Your threshing and mine is not in the hands of men, nor is it in the hands of the devil. Satan may sift us as wheat, but he shall never thresh us as fitches. His foul breath may blow the chaff away, but he will never take possession of the corn. The ancients used to say it like this, "The divine decree leaves nothing to chance. Not a stroke of providence is left to chance." That is why when common temptations assail us, it is always the Lord, Himself, Who makes the way of escape for us.

No chastening seems to be joyous but is grievous to bear. To be sure, threshing is not a pleasant process. I've been switched and I've been beaten and neither one is very pleasant. But I can tell you this much, I am what I am today because of the threshings I've been through. It has yielded the peaceable fruit of righteousness in my life.

If God is threshing you right now, you can be sure of two things. He knows which instrument to use, and he chooses the time and place to use it. He will not thresh you with an unnecessary instrument at an unnecessary time in an unnecessary place. God always exercises discretion.

The husbandman may be zealous in beating out the corn, but he is never abusive. The threshing is limited. He is zealous to beat out the seed, but he is even more careful not to break it into pieces by too severe a process. His wheel is not designed to grind but only to thresh. The horse's feet are not meant to break, only to separate. The cumin is not meant to be crushed, nor fitches fractured. God's chastening is measured. He will never allow you to be tempted above that which you are able to bear. And God will never apply a needless stroke to your life.

Under the Old Law, there was a limit to the number of stripes a man could receive upon his back. If he was beaten for a crime, the law applied "forty stripes save one." In all of our scourging, there is always a limit: a "save one" clause. We do not have to endure a superfluity of threshing. If we have a hundred troubles, it is only because ninety-nine others have failed to produce what is needed. The bread corn is bruised but never broken. Why? Because that is all that is needed for it to produce its very best.

That brings us the good news we need to hear. The threshing is not permanent. Isaiah said, "The bread corn is bruised, but he shall not thresh it forever." In one place the Lord said, "For a small moment

I have forsaken thee, but with great mercies will I gather thee." No matter how angry we think God is, we can be assured that, "He will not always chide nor keep his anger forever." We may have wept bitterly for many long hours, but we know this, "Weeping may endure for the night, but joy is coming in the morning." Our tears are temporary.

It seems less than true, but threshing is not necessary to the corn all year round. The truth is the flail is most often idle. The good always outweighs the bad, and right will always triumph over wrong. There is some rain, but there is more sunshine than storm. There is some pain, but there is more health than there is harm. There is some sorrow, but there is more laughter than there is sadness.

You may be bruised, but you will never be broken.

## *Chapter Fourteen*

# Slain But Certain

> Though he slay me, yet will I trust in him: but I will maintain mine own ways before him.
>
> Job 13:15

The Book of Job is considered one of the greatest literary masterpieces of the Old Testament. It really concerns itself with the inadequacy of worldly standards of happiness and righteousness. Yet the suffering of Job is so overwhelming and so magnificently expressed that it takes precedence over the entire writing.

It was so great that even with our foreknowledge of its purpose and its meaning, it still seems a little excessive. It wasn't Job who had anything to prove, it was actually God. It was God who brought Job up in conversation with the devil. It wasn't Job who got into a debate with the devil about how righteous he was, it was God. To prove His confidence in Job, God took down the hedge He had built around him. As we listen to one messenger after another bring more and more bad news, we wonder, did God really have to go so far just to prove the devil wrong?

The chord of suffering weaves its way throughout the Scripture.

Adam and Eve suffered a great fall. Moses suffered a fatal error. David suffered a terrible mistake. Many more suffered due to their own lack of integrity. These are they which seemed to deserve suffering, for who could expect such disobedience to go unrewarded?

Then there are those who suffered without an apparent just cause. Joseph was despised by his brethren because he was favored by his father. He suffered slavery, exile, accusation, and imprisonment—even though he had done the right things. And somehow, throughout the course of his life, Joseph always possessed the patient ability to simply turn these misfortunes into something positive.

In one horrifying day, a series of calamities struck upon the life of Job like hammer blows landing one on top of the other. Suddenly his wealth disappears, and then without warning his family is gone. Job is smitten with a loathsome disease. He is not like Joseph; Job is an older man. He cannot simply adapt himself to the situation and rise above the circumstances. His loss is so great that he doesn't even want to live.

There is only one thing that keeps him going—he wants to understand the reason for his suffering. For his friends, the answer is simple. Blinded by the fallible standards of the world in which they live, Job's friends are certain that all of the misfortune must be the result of some wickedness in Job's life. Their arguments are based on the worldly notion that success equals virtue.

They attempt to undermine Job's faith, not in God, but in himself. It is difficult to make a convincing argument against God but very easy to sway a man into believing that his troubles are his own fault. It is hard to question God, but to question the integrity of a man is easy enough. So Eliphaz vore dire's his witness, attempting to get Job to speak the truth. "Who ever perished being innocent?" he asks. "Where were the righteous ever cut off?" he ponders aloud.

The experts continue their questioning as other members of this prosecution take their places. Bildad insensitively suggests that perhaps Job is paying for the sins of his children. Without regard for Job's loss, without conscience and full of malice, he suggests that Job's kids were simply the cause for the suffering of their father. Next, Zophar cross examines the witness, turning to prior arguments that perhaps Job was not the man that everyone thought him to be. With great intensity and deep personal conviction, he argues that Job must have indeed sinned or he would not be suffering so greatly.

But Job knows something that these men don't— they are wrong. Job cannot ask forgiveness because there is nothing to be forgiven. He cannot undo something a mistake that wasn't made. There isn't even any indication that his kids were in any way at fault. Eliphaz, Bildad, and Zophar simply missed the mark. They operate under the impression that a man is guilty until proven innocent. If he's on trial then he must have committed the crime.

It is interesting that at this point we know more than Job does about the reason for his suffering. Bear in mind that Job still has no idea as to why any of this is happening. While the reason for it is given to us in the opening two chapters of the story, Job is still in the dark until nearly the end. These first two chapters introduce us to the cause for Job's trial.

God intends to use Job as a demonstration to a skeptical Satan. He intends to show the devil that a human being can retain faith in God and His justice even in the face of the greatest imaginable suffering. God's entire case rests upon this one man. Many people lost their confidence in Job (his own wife and his three friends), but God never did.

We know that Job suffered not because he has sinned but precisely because of his outstanding virtue. But Job doesn't know that. Instead, he is urged to repent of things that he has not done, to take the low road, to learn humility. Just curse God and die! It all seems like an easy way out, and it would be if that were the cause for his trouble.

Job refuses the easy way out because he is full of conviction about his own innocence. No matter what his friends think, Job fully believes that his heart is right with God. His confidence in himself is not pride but pure honesty. He realizes that the problem is much harder to understand than his friends can even imagine. Perhaps taking their advice might lessen his burden, but his conviction will not let him yield.

Job has believed the illogical and accepted a paradox. It is illogical to think that the righteous could surely suffer. It is a paradox to consider that suffering and innocence could go hand in hand. Yet that is exactly the thing that Job clings to.

It is in this state of mind that he proclaims some of the most quoted words in all of human history. "Though he slay me, yet will I trust in Him: but I will maintain mine own ways before him." He is slain, but he is also certain. Job declares that he may be slain of the Lord, but he will also maintain his innocence before the very face of God.

It is one thing to shout, "I'll see you in court!" It is quite a different matter altogether to actually have a case. Job sums up his argument with a detailed account of his righteous ways. He knows that he has done nothing worthy of such agony and pain, therefore, he is determined to stand upon his own integrity. So convincing was his argument that it silenced his three friends. The Bible said, "they ceased to answer Job, because he was righteous in his own eyes."

Let me try to help you. You've heard it said that it's okay to not be okay. Well, it's also okay to believe that you are okay. Some people can't get better because they are convinced of some wrong they supposedly committed. When something bad happens they adopt an attitude that says, "It must be my fault." This perceived fault brings a heavy sense of guilt. They have a difficult time being free because they can't let themselves feel free. There are those that I love and care about that I want to see unburdened of their guilt and shame. They don't have to carry it around, but they do, and it grieves me deeply. They allow someone else's judgement of their character determines the whole tenor of their life. The best thing you can do is to free yourself from any sense of failure that doesn't really exist. Loose yourself from the fetters of unmerited fault.

Too many times we are just like Job's three friends. We have seen too much, heard too much, and believed too easily that conventional wisdom is always right. Living in this old world has rubbed the edges of our minds with such force that the sharpness of our thinking has been dulled. Let us not follow a pattern of thinking that says, "If something bad happens, someone must've done something wrong." Sometimes, it's just life. And on occasion God is allowing us to go through trial just to prove His confidence in us. Job was trusted with tragedy. Perhaps that's why you're facing your own difficulties—God trusts you!

Eliphaz, Bildad, and Zophar not only lost confidence in humanity, they essentially lost confidence in God. They did not believe that a man could honestly live an upright life. They did not know what to think about Job. All they could conclude was that he was not who they thought he was and that God was openly punishing him for being a fraud. They were in no position to speak for God. Their faith was limited to the belief that He was narrow-minded and only punished people for wrongdoings. In their minds, bad things only happened to bad people. These men totally missed the fact that God could so consume a man that that man could live a morally clean life. Job's friends could not fathom that God had the power to sustain him during a time of great tragedy - to show how strong his faith could be, and to reveal the restorative power of God. So, the Lord rebuked them and said, "My wrath is kindled against thee because thou hast spoken things against me that are not right."

Job had been tried, but he was still true. He was true to his convictions. He was true to God. He was true to his family. He was even true to his friends. Just as importantly, he was true to himself.

He was slain, but he was certain. He was certain that he was blameless; that he had not transgressed any laws. He was convinced that his kids were not the cause of his troubles. He was confident that God would give him an audience. He was resolute that God would restore him.

Job's confession caused God to reply. Out of the whirlwind God spoke to him, still not giving him a full explanation of his suffering. Yet, it was a triumphant proclamation of God's power and of His justice. This silences Job, who accepts it in faith.

That God does not reveal the key to the riddle even to the man who has victoriously stood the test and vindicated God's faith in humanity is perhaps the most significant point in the story. It suggests that there is not and never will be an explanation of human suffering that our intelligence can comprehend.

Sufferers, like Job, must cling to their faith in themselves and in God. There are simply times when we must accept the fact that our own inexplicable suffering is somehow connected to the working of God's divine justice. That all things are working for our good. That God will perfect that which concerns you. There comes a time when all of us will have to say, "Though he slay me yet will I trust in him." The real question however, is can you say, "I will maintain mine own ways before Him. I may be slain, but I am certain that God will work it all out in the end."

## *Chapter Fifteen*

# Leafless But Not Lifeless

> Then said I, Lord, how long? And he answered, Until the cities be wasted without inhabitant, and the houses without man, and the land be utterly desolate, And the Lord have removed men far away, and there be a great forsaking in the midst of the land. But yet in it shall be a tenth, and it shall return, and shall be eaten: as a teil tree, and as an oak, whose substance is in them, when they cast their leaves: so the holy seed shall be the substance thereof.
>
> Isaiah 6:11-13

Isaiah has just had an incredible encounter with the Lord. King Uzziah has died. Grief has stricken the nation. The prophet is awash with sorrow and yet he finds himself in awe of God's presence. "In the year King Uzziah died," says Isaiah, "I saw also the Lord sitting upon a throne, high and lifted up, and his train filled the temple" (Is. 6:1). He witnesses seraphim as they minister unto the Lord. Each of them had six wings, "with twain they covered their face, with twain they covered their feet and with twain they did fly" (Is. 6:2). As they moved about the throne of God, they cried out to each other saying, "Holy, holy, holy, is the Lord of hosts: the whole earth is full of his glory" (Is. 6:3). Their worship was so powerful that it shook the pillars and the posts of the temple wherein Isaiah stood. Smoke began to arise with the Sanctuary, an indication of the rising wrath of God. Such a sight moved him and made him acutely aware of his own perilous condition. Then Isaiah cried, "Woe is me! for I am undone; because I am a man of unclean lips, and I dwell in the midst of a people of unclean lips: for mine eyes have seen the King, the Lord of hosts" (Is. 6:5). By the hand of an angel his lips are touched with a live coal from heaven's altar. This purging produced the preserving of his words and performed the cleansing of his conversation so that his message is forever emblazoned upon the souls of men.

I am amazed by the fact that many of history's greatest warnings were often ignored by those to whom they were given. On the night of April 14, 1912, the banquet halls and decks of the Titanic were alive with excitement. On its maiden voyage the heralded vessel was headed straight for disaster. It's two radio operators, Jack Phillips and Harold Bride were overwhelmed by passengers sending and receiving telegrams while on board the famous ship. In the hectic hours of that frigid night several warnings were sent to the Titanic. Other vessels were reporting icebergs and fields of ice in the vicinity of the Titanic. Jack and Harold passed these warnings on to the bridge, and while it seems that Captain Edward J. Smith did alter his course slightly, he never slowed the ship's speed.

For the most part, he either ignored or did not take seriously the warnings that had been given. After all, his ship was unsinkable. But his failure to heed the warnings resulted in one of the worst maritime tragedies in history. 1500 lives were lost when the Titanic struck an iceberg in the Northern Atlantic.

It mattered not to Israel how anointed the lips of the prophet were. They hardly seem to pay Isaiah any notice. If they did alter their course, it was only slightly, and they never slowed down. They were determined to continue in their sin. And this they did until the wrath of God nearly consumed them.

It prompted Isaiah to ask, "How long? O, Lord!" "How long will this people remain impenitent?" "How long will they continue in their sin?" "How long will your judgment be upon them?" (Is. 6:11). The news he received was not good. He was informed that God would waste and destroy the cities and their inhabitants until the land should be utterly desolate.

The Lord said, "In it there shall be a tenth that will return" (Is. 6:13). Historians tell us that this remnant did, in fact, return. In 597 BC, Nebuchadnezzar led the people into Babylonian captivity. There was a group of the poorest Israelites left behind to serve as "farmers and vinedressers" (II Kings 25:12). However, this remnant was also subjected to the prophecy of Isaiah. The Lord said, "It shall return and shall be eaten" (Is. 6:13). When this small number of people had been nearly devoured there were still some that remained who escaped to Egypt only to be cut off and perish in a strange land (II Kings 25:26).

Here is the hope in Isaiah's prophecy. God said, "Although only this tenth shall be preserved and then even this small part shall be subjected to many perils, yet Israel shall not be destroyed, for it shall be as a teal tree and as an oak." When these trees lose their leaves and appear to be dead, they are much alive because their substance is within them. So, this remnant, riddled with death and plagued with peril doesn't appear to have much life and yet, it is very much alive because its substance is within it. It contains a holy seed that cannot die. When the land is desolate it will spring to life. When the land is arid, when drought persists, there is a holy substance that will saturate and supply it. Even if the tree is cut down there is still hope. Job said, "For there is hope of a tree, if it be cut down, that it will sprout again, and that the tender branch thereof will not cease"(Job 14:7).

This promise was primarily spoken to the Jewish people. There is no nation on earth with a more colorful and checkered history than Israel. No group of people in the world can more specifically trace their lineage than the Jews. As a race, they can trace their roots all the way back to Abraham and from Abraham to Noah and from Noah to Adam. Their heritage spans the course of human history with great accuracy and detail.

No other nation has suffered at the hands of their enemies like Israel. Nebuchadnezzar destroyed their temple. He left no stone standing upon another and then dragged them off into captivity. The remaining tenth was brutalized and beaten until nothing much of them remained. Yet in time, they rose from their ashes like a phoenix and built another Temple and became strong as a nation once again. Though often assaulted and desolated they have withstood and abide still today. So that the words of an old prophet came to pass, "the scepter did not depart from Judah nor a lawgiver from between his feet."

Mighty waves have crashed upon their shores and yet they stand as a great nation in our generation. Emperors have razed their most sacred temples to the ground. Conquerors have renamed their most holy cities and forbidden them to stand upon their most sacred soils. Yet, Israel stands today.

In more recent history, the nation gained its right to exist and immediately those who sought and still seek its complete annihilation have come against it. I read that the state of Israel is only forty miles wide at one point. It is surrounded by massive nations like Egypt, Syria, Iran, Iraq and Saudi Arabia. In 1947, when the United Nations voted to establish a national home for the Jews it was rejected by the Arab nations. Their leader, Haj Amin al_Hussaini, declared a "holy war" and sent out a decree to "murder them all!" On the day Israel declared its independence Egypt, Syria, Iraq, Jordan and Lebanon amassed their armies and attacked the tiny nation. But Israel defeated them. In 1956, Israel survived the Syrian War. In 1967, they survived the Six Day War. In 1973, they survived the Yom Kippur War. On October 7, 2023, more than 1,200 men, women and children, including 46 Americans and citizens of more than 30 countries, were slaughtered by Hamas – the largest massacre of Jews since the Holocaust. For over two years, Israel has been engaged in a bloody battle with a perpetual enemy.

In every subsequent missile attack, terrorist plot and the rejection of other countries Israel has remained a strong and vibrant nation. As we pray for the peace of Jerusalem and the posterity of the nation of Israel, we are reminded that its substance is within it. There is holy seed within its national core. Mark my words well, "No matter what happens Israel will survive." God is on its side! "If God is for it who can be against it?"

When God places His sustaining substance within something, it will never be destroyed. I believe that God has placed a holy seed within the Church. Through the ages the Church has been ravaged and pillaged, but it stands stronger today than ever before. There have been times when it looked like there was a great forsaking in the midst of the land, but the Church was preserved. As a tree of life, the Church has been found to sometimes appear barren and leafless. Yet, it has remained because its substance is within it. Its enemies have assaulted and persecuted it, but the Church has grown all the more. Men have marred its message and tampered with its teachings, but its truth is declared triumphantly today. The devil has ransacked it and wreaked havoc upon it, but the gates of hell have not prevailed against it. False doctrine has invaded its precepts and principles, but the Word of God remains forever settled. Truth has fallen in the streets, but it has risen up again. The flood of humanistic thinking couldn't drown out the Church. The fires of heretical zeal couldn't eradicate its banners. Persecution drove its followers into the catacombs, but deeper in their devotion.

The Church has been stripped bare of its leaves throughout history. It has been robbed of its purity at times. It has been prostituted to the desires and agendas of men. The Church has been silenced for centuries at a time, driven from pillar to post. It has been uprooted and transplanted into soil not fit for its fruitfulness. To put it bluntly, there have been times when the Church didn't look like much. It looked like it had little to offer; little to give. It seemed of no benefit to anyone, appearing to be dead. Its revelations were few and far between, causing its revival spirit to look as if it was a thing of the past.

Yet the Church still stands today. It's been through it all, seen it all, experienced it all and yet it still stands strong in this generation. Why? How? The answer is simple. Its substance is within it. It's been battered and beaten and yet the Old Ship of Zion sails on. There is more substance within than there is storm without. Every unholy action has been carried out against, or even in the name of, the Church, yet it remains vibrant in a cold world. There is a holy seed within it that no unholy pestilence can eradicate.

God's presence abides within His Church. Wherever God is, there is life. Even if it looks like there are just a handful of people involved in it the Church is a powerful force in a community because it is compassed about by a great cloud of witnesses. As long as God's Spirit is alive and well within the Church nothing can keep it from growing. Sometimes the Church is pruned. Sometimes it gets some bark knocked off of it, cut back so much that it looks like it will never rebound and produce anything fruitful ever again. But it does because it has substance in it.

The Church grows numerically because I'm in it and you are in it. But it thrives because God's Spirit is in it. It was just a remnant, but God raised it up. It had a substance that produced life. It may look leafless, but it has never been lifeless.

And what more shall I say concerning the child of God? Are we not all trees of righteousness; the planting of the Lord? Jeremiah said that men who put their trust in the Lord are, "As a tree planted by the waters, and that spreadeth out its roots by the river, and shall not see when heat cometh, but its leaf shall be green; and shall not be careful in the year of drought, neither shall cease from yielding fruit" (Jer. 17:8).

The teal tree Isaiah referred to was an evergreen. When we hear that we assume that it never lost its leaves or that they never lost their color. But in certain inclement conditions the teal tree did, in fact, lose its leaves or at least its color. It reminds us that even in the godliest of lives there are seasons when the color fades or the leaf withers. There are times of trial that bring a certain look of death to the tree.

We've all been there. Maybe you are there now. You don't appear to be profitable or prosperous. You don't seem to have much to offer anyone, or anything to give. Your face is drawn, your vision is dimmed, and you appear to be lifeless. Your leaf has withered, or at the very least is anything but a vibrant green. But you are not dead. There is substance within you.

How many times have God's people been afflicted and yet the more they were afflicted the more they grew and multiplied. Pressure turned to expansion. Hardship became a catalyst for prosperity. Persecution magnified their blessing. God's people have been sawn asunder, forced to live in caves and dens of the earth, pursued and put to flight but they are still standing strong in their faith. Elijah bows his head and says, "I'm the only one left standing!" But God says, "No! I still have seven thousand whose substance is in them and they haven't bowed either!" Jesus handpicks twelve men to carry out His mission after He is gone and everyone of them in some way fall into a state of leaflessness. Peter says, "I'm going fishing." But when Jesus shows up, He sends him out as a "fisher of men." It looked like Peter was finished after he denied the Lord. You talk about losing it; Peter lost it. But on the day of Pentecost, he stood strong because there was substance within him.

Do you feel like you have lost everything? You feel like you've been stripped bare of your joy, your faith, your anointing and even your purpose. You look like a leafless tree. Your faith has faded, your hope is halted, your hands hang down, your eyes are dimmed, and you can barely stand on your feeble knees. But I want to tell you something. "You have substance within you." There is a holy seed within that is waiting to burst forth with life. That pressure within is life attempting to produce itself without. Greater is that which is in you than that which is around you.

You may be in a storm but you're not going to sink because there is substance within. Take inventory of those you admire and look up to. There are people who have been through severe trial, but they are still standing. There are some who have felt like quitting, but they are still conquering. Some felt like turning back a long time ago, yet they continue to move forward. There are others who looked like they would never do much for God, but they are soul winners today. Time fails us to tell of the tragedies and heartaches they have seen. We could not enumerate on the instances when Satan attacked them with all his might. We cannot begin to know the secret storms and struggles they have gone through. But here they are. They may look leafless, but they are not lifeless.

Don't count that tree out whose branches are bare, who gives the impression of deadness. Don't cut it down just yet. Several years ago, I was given a peach tree to plant on my property. It was just a stick, really, with just a few small branches on it. I tried really hard to protect it – to keep someone from riding a four-wheeler over it. Try as I might, one day I noticed the little tree was bent over. When I inspected it, my suspicion was confirmed. It was barely standing between two tire tracks. I started to just pull it up by its roots, but I remembered what Job said about the hope of a tree. So, I tenderly stood it back upright, secured it with a stake for support and cared for it over the next few months. To my surprise, when spring arrived that little tree budded. It had substance after all.

Sometimes we look so barren because the world looks so fruitful, but I remind you that David said, "When the workers of iniquity flourish, it is they that shall be cut off forever." Yet on the other hand… "The righteous shall flourish like a palm tree, he shall grow like a cedar in Lebanon. Those that be planted in the house of the Lord shall flourish in the courts of our God." Just because we are leafless doesn't mean we are lifeless.

Stir up the gift of God inside of you. Stir up the substance of the Spirit that indwells your life. You may be in the storm, but it doesn't have to be in you.

# Just One More Thing...

Hang in there! The tables are going to turn. Favor is coming upon you. God has not forgotten you. Your mourning is turning into dancing, your sorrow into joy. Lamentation has its limitation. Weeping endures, but only for the night.

As I close this little book, the thought occurs to me that many more chapters could be written. Perhaps they will. Who knows? What I can tell you is that while you may be down, you are not out. You may be troubled but don't be in despair.

In John Bunyan's famous allegory, Pilgrim's Progress, Christian is traveling toward the Palace Beautiful when he sees two lions standing on either side of a very narrow passage. It was here that many travelers became overwhelmed by fear and turned back. Christian is just about to do the same when he hears the voice of the "porter of the lodge" call out to him. "Fear not the lions, for they are chained, and are placed there for trial of faith," he said. Thus encouraged, Christian followed the porter's directions and made it safely between the lions to his destination.

I feel like that porter. I just want to encourage someone so they can make it all the way through to their destination. Don't give up. Don't turn back now. You've come this far by faith. Don't go home in fear. Look closer. The lions are chained! They can roar, but they can't reach. They are there only to reveal your faith.

www.ingramcontent.com/pod-product-compliance
Lightning Source LLC
LaVergne TN
LVHW010931110826
845149LV00013B/2548
* 9 7 8 1 9 6 1 4 8 2 2 5 8 *